# The Chemical Conquistador: Colonel North & His Nitrate Dream House

## Roberta Woods

The Chemical Conquistador: Colonel North & His Nitrate
Dream House

Copyright ©2020 Roberta Woods

Layout and Design by JingotheCat.com - Andy Grachuk

# Contents

# Image Credits

Image 1: Bywater Street, Leeds (circa 1959) — by permission of Leeds Digital Image Library

Image 2: Map of Leeds 1890 — Alan Godfrey Maps (with author's annotation)

Image 3: North goes native - 'Colonel John T. North, The Nitrate King' Harpers Weekly Feb 6 1892

Image 4: Liverpool Nitrate Co. Oficina — Melton Prior's illustrations for 'A Visit to Chile'

Image 5: Men Working Primitiva Nitrate Fields - Melton Prior's illustrations for 'A Visit to Chile'

Image 6: Portrait of the King - author's copy RRC Gregory's 'Story of Royal Eltham'

Image 7: Emma on the terrace at Avery Hill — courtesy of UOG archives

Image 8: The North party on the deck of the Galicia - Melton Prior's illustrations for 'A Visit to Chile'

Image 9: Whyte's Hotel Tijuca (Rio de Janeiro) - Melton Prior's illustrations for 'A Visit to Chile'

Image 10: Colonel & Emma, Cauquenes, Chile - Melton Prior's illustrations for 'A Visit to Chile'

Image 11: Nitrate Railways Iquique, Chile - Melton Prior's illustrations for 'A Visit to Chile'

Image 12: Primitiva oficina - Melton Prior's illustrations for 'A Visit to Chile'

Image 13: Hotel Metropole, London advertisement (author's own) / Menu — courtesy of UOG archives

Image 14: Jane & Emma North - courtesy of UOG archives

Image 15: Aerial view of Avery Hill College (1920's, 30?) — author's own

# Chronology

1842 – John Thomas North born in Holbeck , Leeds

1869 – North leaves for Peru as an employee of Fowler's Steam Plough & Locomotive Works

1871 – Has left Fowler's and is working in his first nitrate plant as an engineer

1875 – Branches out by himself into water supply by investing and converting an old steamer, he also has railway interests and is expanding his nitrate interests. North secures government contract for the supply of water

1879-83 – War of the Pacific, North takes opportunity to buy nitrate certificates (bearer bonds) at rock-bottom prices due to political instability

1882 – Returns from South America and proceeds to exploit his nitrate holdings on the stock exchange through joint-stock companies

1882 – 89 Nitrate Boom years but North diversifies into railways

1883-88 – North takes out a 10 year lease on Avery Hill at £550 pa for the existing house from Mrs Boyd after the death of her husband

1888 – Having met the architect T.W.Cutler at the Italian Exhibition in London, North begins to entertain the idea of building a large Italianate mansion and in December of that year persuades Mrs Boyd to sell him the existing house and thirty seven acre estate for the sum of £17,500 according to David Shorney - Edmundson states £17,000.

1889 – North commissions Cutler to undertake 'additions and alterations' to the house which the architect calculates at £40,000, a sum which is rapidly revised to £65,000 by the architect. However, North soon discovered that Cutler had embarked into contracts with builders and interior decorators totalling some £100,000 (Jill Franklin is very specific in quoting £99,396 as being cost to 1890). Cutler was promptly sacked and the works completed by his assistant J.O.Cook. The Builder Dec 18th 1909 pg 678 says expenditure on Avery Hill was between £250,000 - £300,000! Monetary equivalence - £20,000 in 1890 would equal £2,000,000 today

1889 – Final Trip to Chile

1890 – Works on Avery Hill completed later this year

1891 – Litigation Cutler v North relating to building costs

1896 – North dies suddenly at the early age of 54 leaving in his will some £700,000 (gross?) according to Shorney- Edmundson states £453,091, excluding any property overseas, which belies accounts of North having lost the bulk of his fortune by this time. Family decide to sell Avery Hill

1898 – Alonzo Stocker, a celebrated psychiatrist buys the house and 140 acre estate for a paltry £40,000. Whatever his plans may have been, tragically, the mansion was to remain empty for a further 8 years as Stocker never actually took up residence.

1902 – Stocker sells the mansion and 84 acres of parkland to the then London County Council for the sum of £25,000, just a few thousand more than North had paid for the original house before proceeding to spend £200,000+ on it!

1940's – House suffers slight incendiary bomb damage but is then left unoccupied for a further 5+ years with the result that all of the eastern wing, except the Lavatory was demolished and now all that remains of North's 50-room mansion are the entrance hall, ornate lavatory, library, drawing room, ballroom and miraculously the mini Crystal Palace of the Winter Gardens

1992 – Avery Hill sold by Greenwich Council to University of Greenwich for knock-down price of £1!

2019 – UOG agree to pass responsibility for the upkeep of the Winter Garden to Greenwich Council at the same time as selling the remaining grounds and the Mansion to Harris Academy for a boy's secondary school. There are ongoing objections to this from local residents.

# Introduction

On a cold February evening in 1891, Eltham residents may have noticed a succession of grand carriages as they made their way down the High Street and along the newly-diverted Bexley road from the London direction, bound for Colonel North's recently completed mansion at Avery Hill. One such conveyance, was that of Baron Nathan Mayer de Rothschild and his wife Emma and inside the occupants were engrossed in conversation:

'My dear', declared the Baron 'I have to confess I have some reservations about North, he seems a rather brash and ostentatious individual, and just recently managed to annoy the POW considerably with his over-familiarity at the Newmarket races. He has even acquired the title 'Colonel,' and to my knowledge, the man has never seen a day's military service active or otherwise'

'As you say Natty, he does appear to be typical of that new breed, who seek to 'ape' their betters, nevertheless, I have heard reports that he has spared no expense on this new house of his and I for one, shall be intrigued to see what he has managed to do with it, although I am sure it is no match for our own dear Tring Park' replied the Baroness

*'However' ventured the Baron 'I have to admit a sneaking admiration for our host, his fortune has been achieved by his own earnest endeavour, while mine has come down the line with the House of Rothschild, and yours, my dear, when you were lucky enough to catch the eye of yours truly'*

*Emma looked at her husband, raised her eyebrows and smiled.*

*Their carriage now turned right off the road and proceeded under the splendid 'Prince of Wales Entrance', so named as the Colonel had every hope, that in time, he could attract the heir to the throne to his new palace. As their carriage passed through the ornate red-brick archway with its 15ft high wrought-iron gates displaying Norths intertwined initials, Emma winced noticing the newly acquired coat of arms – how vulgar! Alas, she feared, the prince himself would not be gracing the 'Jolly' Colonel with his presence this evening, although appearing quite happy availing himself of the Colonel's munificence when he saw fit. What could not be disputed, was the Colonel's reputation for providing an excellent evening's entertainment and this one promised to be exceptional. The Colonel's invitation was to a 'musical evening', but this was essentially an opportunity for all those interested, to have a peek at the recently completed refurbishment of his Mansion, which some say cost a staggering £200,000.*

*The house itself now came into view, a long, low, house, not overly ostentatious on the outside, but early reports said magnificently appointed on the inside, by all accounts. The brilliant new-fangled electric light emanated from the top-windows of the ballroom, illuminating the way for the carriages as they proceeded towards main entrance under the imposing port-cochére, where a group of liveried North footmen awaited their arrival. Colonel North had summoned the 'great and the good' along with family, friends and business acquaintances to a soiree, his first opportunity to show off his newly completed mansion and it promised to be an eventful evening.*

Fast-forward to the current year, and the view of Avery Hill presented to the newcomer on entering through that same gateway, has changed radically. Gone is the vista of the *long low house,* the smallest details of which North and his architect Cutler had laboured long and hard over (producing over one thousand preparatory drawings), and on which only the finest materials had been used. Utilitarian educational buildings erected since the house became a women's college in 1908, now obscure what is left of a once *state of the art* gentleman's residence, more than half of which was demolished due to neglect following bomb damage during WW2 – the result being, the impossibility of visualising the house as it was in 1890. Meanwhile, as I write, the University of Greenwich have sold the whole Mansion site which is set to become a Harris Academy boy's school, a purpose for which, in 2019 it is totally unfit, as it was in 1902 when the LCC mooted a similar usage, having acquired the property. Greenwich Council seem to have undertaken some responsibility for maintaining the Winter Garden but what future awaits the remains of the Mansion itself, only parts of which are listed, remains unclear. This property, which was always intended to be partly open to the public, now faces a most uncertain future.

Contrast Avery Hill's sad slide into dereliction with the phoenix-like resurrection of nearby Eltham Palace, which since it's renovation in the late 1990's, has become a place of pilgrimage for many who delight in its unique setting and lavish Art-Deco interiors complete with moat and medieval hall. Few of these culture-vultures will be aware of its neglected poor relation, the Avery Hill Mansion which lies less than one mile away on the Bexley Road. And yet, our intrepid Colonel was busy throwing piles of cash at the construction of his own mini-palace, some forty years before the Courtaulds began their transformation of Eltham Palace. In the last decade of the 19thC, while the great hall of Eltham Palace was reduced to being used as a cattle-shed, having descended into neglect and disrepair over several centuries, the Colonel was laying on three special train carriages to transport 1000 guests to Eltham Station (opened in 1866, this is what is now Mottingham Station), where a fleet of horse-drawn vehicles would be waiting to ferry them to one of his famously lavish soirees at the Mansion, as described in my imagined opening paragraph.

It is truly a tragedy that North's Victorian extravaganza of a house has not survived intact, as had it done so, it would have made a fitting foil for the more restrained art-deco splendour of the neighbouring Palace and as I write, another chapter in the tragedy looms as the University of Greenwich (who have already presided over a slide into dereliction of the Winter Garden) prepares to leave the Mansion site in *2019* without having secured it's future, with the remains of the house facing being boarded-up and the Winter Garden, potentially turning into a health and safety issue with its Canarian palm trees set to push through the roof of the glass-house for want of pruning. Luckily, a local group has got together under the banner *Save Avery Hill Winter Garden* and having caught the attention of celebrity gardeners like Alan Titchmarch and Tom Hart-Dyke (Lullingstone World Garden) it now seems to be attracting a little publicity as South-East London's '*Kew*' or even '*Crystal Palace*'. In fact Colonel North's house had already been described as '*New Eltham Palace*' in an article shortly after its completion, in the Express of Aug. 9 1890.

Most Eltham residents will know of the Winter Garden at Avery Hill even if they have not heard of its illustrious creator. They may even have been there on a school trip or for a walk with their parents. However, many, myself included, remained ignorant of the Mansion itself, of which the Winter Garden was just a part. Hearing about the Campaign to Save the Winter Garden and then reading about the red marble-lined and onyx-pillared library, prompted a wish to know more of this fascinating house and it's equally fascinating creator, John Thomas North, or *Colonel North* as he came to be popularly known.

It is difficult to arrive at a true appraisal of the Colonel, as many of the contemporary accounts, anecdotes and newspaper articles portray him as a puffed-up, self-important, cartoon-like figure. Depending on who you are reading, he may *be millionaire adventurer, lovable rogue, ruthless swindler* or *generous benefactor.* And aside from Edmundson's book '*Colonel North: The Nitrate King*', which is not strictly a biography, but more an academic account of the nitrate industry in Chile, there is very little other than the newspaper articles written about our man during his lifetime. Many of these contemporary newspaper articles were spurious *spoofs* written to entertain rather than inform the reader – they might be likened to the fake news and clickbait that bedevil our current media. Some stories are so unlikely as to be easily discounted, others may just hold a grain of truth to those familiar with the Colonel's playful nature and tendency to court publicity.

While he was not decorated by his own nation, either while alive or posthumously, no fewer than four foreign nations conferred honours upon the Colonel in recognition of public services. The Khedive of Egypt made him '*Commander of the Imperial Order of Osmanich*', the King of the Belgians (he whose statues are now being destroyed by 'progressives') awarded him '*The Order of The Lion, First Class*' a similar order to that conferred on Sir Henry Stanley explorer (Dr Livingstone , I presume). France gave him the 'Order of Merit' and from the King of Italy he received '*The Second Class Order of Umberto*' (although I have yet to come across any activities in Italy) maybe it was as a patron of Italian arts or more probably, the Colonel being President of the Reception Committee of the Italian Exhibition in 1888, which gave him the idea for building his Mansion in the *Italianate* style. Highfield House built 1869 in Gloucestershire and Queen Victoria's beloved Osborne House on the Isle of Wight are good examples of this architectural style which sought to emulate the Italian Renaissance palazzo.

On a visit to Harrogate, which is just outside North's birthplace in Leeds, I was struck by the fact that it had a rather lavish Victorian Royal Baths including a Turkish Bath and Winter Garden which got me thinking that maybe Colonel North got his inspiration there, until I discovered that these were opened in 1897 after the Colonel's premature death in 1896. Perhaps it was the other way round, and Richard Ellis, Mayor of Harrogate 1884-1887, '*father of Victorian Harrogate*' and promoter of the idea of a grand bathing and hydrotherapy centre, may have been a guest at Avery Hill as there was every possibility that the two self-made Yorkshiremen, would have been known to one another.

North's reputation as an archetypal Victorian '*robber baron*', has ensured that his memory has slipped into that black memory hole reserved for those that are judged by current mores to be unworthy of remembrance. Currently, no historic figure is safe from a revisionist assessment of their contribution to posterity and had a memorial been erected to the Colonel, we can be sure there would be those who would be clamouring to have it removed, as they are currently doing with Cecil Rhodes, King Leopold II of Belgium (he who had decorated the good Colonel), American Confederate Generals - the list is endless. We might also pause to reflect that those same dubious financial practices that the Colonel was accused of have continued throughout the 20th into the 21st century, with insider trading and the creation of highly toxic financial instruments leading to the global financial crash of 2008.

North acquired the honorary title of *Colonel* through his financing of the 2nd Tower Hamlets (East London) Engineer Volunteer Corps in 1885. Cynics might see this as little better than the purchasing of honours, a practise very popular amongst rich men at the time. North was so attached to his military style and apparel, that he was known as *Colonel North* for the remainder of his life. During the 1880's boom years in the nitrate industry, the Colonel acquired another title *The Nitrate King* and invariably, in newspaper accounts he was usually identified using both, '*Colonel North: The Nitrate King*'.

A remarkable Englishman, North rose, in his own words, "*from mechanic to millionaire*" in the space of some twenty years; his activities in the 1880's and 1890's a constant subject of interest to the commercial press, and whose efforts to become a figure in society were almost as dramatic as his manipulation of the nitrate market on the London Stock Exchange. A self-made entrepreneur, endowed with considerable business acumen and an ebullient character, North belongs to the age of Cecil Rhodes and Julius Wernher, though, unlike them, he is almost completely forgotten in his own country. Indeed, while Rhodes and Wernher were busy making their fortunes in the diamond and gold mines of South Africa, North was building his in the nitrate fields of Chile. There are many parallels in the lives of the three men, they were all driven, resourceful and adventurous and all left their home countries at a tender age. Cecil Rhodes was just 11 when he set off from Bishops Stortford, Wernher left Germany aged 21 and North was 27 when he left Leeds for Peru (now Chile), in 1869. All hoped to make their fortunes many thousands of miles from home and all were spectacularly successful in doing so. Julius Wernher's eponymous *Wernher Collection* of priceless antiquities is now housed in the Ranger's House on Blackheath. Like North, Wernher was public spirited and generous and seems to have enjoyed his wealth, although his millions gave him a dread of being introduced to a new person *'lest they should begin to beg from me'* – North had no such dread of the many who made demands on his generosity and was happy to dig deep in his pockets when such occasion arose. Wernher also threw large sums at house renovation - work at his home Luton Hoo in 1905 went way over budget just like North's at Avery Hill.

There was more than a touch of the *nouveau riche arriviste* in North; he continued to claim he was still just a *'country boy made good'*, while simultaneously courting ambitions of being received into *society*. Many socialites, minor aristocrats and their hangers-on would have been keen to avail themselves of North's lavish hospitality while maybe secretly scoffing at his humble origins and general bumptiousness with his honorary military title and all the showy accoutrements of *new* money. However, despite his wealth, the Colonel never sought to deny his Northern roots, proclaiming to all who would listen *'The one pleasure I have in life is to be born a Yorkshireman'*. He did not stint when it came to indulging in his other pleasures like racehorses, greyhounds and ostentatious jewellery and his epitaph *'I have enjoyed myself thoroughly',* proclaims a larger-than-life Fallstaffian character. Indeed, John Benyon

Booth in *'Palmy Days'*, a volume of reminiscences *'of a world that vanished in 1914'*, but mainly of notable characters from Victorian days, observed *'there was a touch of the typical John Bull in the bluff old Colonel's attitude to life'*.

David Shorney (A Brief History of the Mansion....) agrees:-

'he exhibited all the hallmarks of the British character, jingoism and brash self-confidence of the Victorian entrepreneur' 'A bluff, quick-witted Yorkshireman who endeared himself to his contemporaries as much by his jovial and boisterous humour as by his open-handed generosity'

No one could embody the spirit of late Victorian individualism better than North with his jingoistic self-confidence, hallmarks of the British character which were all too soon to disappear with the turn of the century.'

David also showed me an entry for Colonel North in his 1899 edition of *'Chambers Biographical Dictionary'*, a relatively slim book considering it purports to contain anyone of any importance since the beginning of records:-

**'Colonel John Thomas North** (1842-96) 'The Nitrate King' because owner of vast nitrate fields in Tarapaća and of enormous wealth'

So it seems our Colonel is worthy of an entry in this *'Hall of Fame'* and yet is missing from the Eltham *notables* benches recently installed on the High Street. Again, when I visited him, David Shorney also pointed out the opening page of *'Horatio Bottomley - Biography of an Outstanding Personality'* by S. Theodore Felstead published by John Murray 1936:-

'In that long list of picturesque personalities who have flitted across the social, political and commercial life of England in the last fifty years, there have been many men who have achieved widespread fame and notoriety for a brief period and then, like the sky-rockets they were, crashed to earth, never to be seen or heard of again'

The author then goes on to mention a few of these gentlemen, making the most of the astronomical metaphor :-

'Colonel North, commonly known as the 'Nitrate King', who lost on the Stock Exchange, the greater part of the vast fortune he had made out of Chilean nitrates – they were indeed a constellation of stars who sparkled and shone until such time as their ambitious scheme overwhelmed them'.

Perhaps a hard-headed and sometimes ruthless businessman when necessary, the Colonel was nevertheless open-handed and generous to those less fortunate than himself, who were lucky enough to cross his path and on his many travels would always attract a large crowd of petitioners with their hard-luck stories, as tales of his good nature always preceded him. Despite his millions, he did not affect *airs and graces,* his dialogue was liberally sprinkled with '*a bit of racy Yorkshire vernacular*' and he seemed to delight in slyly poking fun at Victorian priggishness. On being reminded by a local '*man of the cloth*' that the previous owner of his house had made his money in sugar, the Colonel was quick to reply '*And I in muck!*' – a reference to nitrate's use as a fertiliser.

One odd discovery during my research, was an American newspaper article dated Aug 18 1987, in the National Enquirer, linking Colonel Oliver North of the Iran/Contras scandal with our own Colonel North – when I first mentioned a link, I was reliably informed that there was none – until I added that this article was in the Avery Hill archive. I came across '*Ollie North's Amazing Roots',* while labouring through the Avery Hill archives up there in the Minstrels Gallery (before they were sent to the UOG Library in Greenwich). Two reporters from the National Enquirer had undertaken to trace Colonel Oliver North's English ancestry, and they seem to have been successful in going back as far as 1400, uncovering several ancestors in Yorkshire. It mentions a distant cousin of *our* North, one Arthur North (1848-1919), a political cartoonist (although I cannot find any reference to him on the internet), and Mary North (born 1700), a common ancestor that they supposedly shared with Colonel Oliver North. This was quite odd in two respects: a) my first internet searches for *Colonel North* repeatedly returned the American variety b) both North's with South American links:- Oliver to Nicaragua and John Thomas to Chile. And here I was now, presented with this indisputable link. However, the article referred to *our* Colonel simply as a '*gambler who had won more than $110,000 at the racecourse*' and they also claimed he '*made millions from bird-droppings*' which is not strictly accurate but made for a more striking headline than *nitrate*.

Having set out on my quest to discover what I could of North and his Mansion, I was most disappointed at the dearth of material available on the subjects in this age of the internet – no photos from the time of the Mansion's completion in 1890, even though I knew these existed – no images at all of the Eastern wing (which held the famed Turkish Bath) and the only book on the subject, William Edmundson's *The Nitrate King*, which is essentially an academic book, coming under *Studies of The Americas* and priced from £40 on Amazon. And all this at a time when the future of the Mansion is under threat. Having been inspired on seeing what remained of the Mansion - the Sculpture Gallery, Picture Gallery/Ballroom, Lavatory and the Winter Garden, I desperately wanted to know more about this extraordinary house and the man who built it.

*Those were the circumstances in which I was prompted to write this account.*

## History of the Avery Hill Site

After the Norman Conquest the land now comprising Avery Hill, was gifted to the King's brother, Bishop Odo. Most of the land remained Crown property until the nineteenth century. There are records from 1290 of King Edward buying hay to feed the starving deer at Eltham Palace, from John de Henley, owner of the fields whose manor house stood there on what is now known as Henley's Field where there are now riding stables. The wider area is known as Pippenhall Meadows, five in number and originally part of Pippenhall Farm - it's hedgerows are believed to be the oldest in Greenwich; the earliest dating back to the 1370's. It is the only London site where pyramidal orchids may be found. The damp central area is caused by a natural spring and a pond and brook which eventually feeds into the River Shuttle. Watercress beds were once fed by this spring.

Adjoining Conduit Meadow is home to a Tudor conduit (Conduit Head) in the north- west corner of the park and this ancient structure supplied fresh water to Eltham Palace. In Elizabethan times Ann Twist, Mistress of the Royal Laundry to Elizabeth 1, owned the fields at Avery Hill. It is possible that this place's name refers to an aviary that may have existed here in the early 19th century.

All of this land was incorporated into the Avery Hill estate in the 1890's by Colonel North.

A map of 1805 calls this area *Pollcat End*. However, in his 1909 book *Royal Eltham*, Gregory refers to the area of the *Crown Woods* that extended in this direction towards Southwood House, as *Pole-Cat End*. These were the royal hunting-grounds and pole-cats would have been high on the gamekeepers list of avowed enemies; they were known to affix the skins of culled cats to nearby trees to deter others and thus the name stuck. One wonders whether the cats were *savvy* enough to read these signs! Gregory goes on to say that Colonel North's house stood within the beautiful park as one proceeded from Pole-Cat End towards Bexley Road. He also mentions that in an auction bill advertising the sale of the house on 19th May 1859, the name was spelt *Aviary* Hill and that it was also spelt in this same manner on one of the tombstones in Eltham churchyard, although I have yet to substantiate this.[1]

---

1   RRC Gregory 'The Story of Royal Eltham' Pgs 284-5 Kentish District Times Company Ltd 1909

In the 19<sup>th</sup> century the first mansions were built at Avery Hill. From 1836 the house here was occupied by Thomas Hale, whose occupation was stated as being a *'proprietor of houses'* according to the 1851 census. Hale was an unmarried gentleman who was living here with his two spinster sisters until his death in 1858 at the age of fifty seven.

Then from 1859 until his death in May 1882 aged seventy-nine, Avery Hill was owned by Glasgow-born sugar merchant James Boyd, whose refinery in Breezer's Hill near St George's-in-the-East in the East End of London, had made him a rich man. Boyd had lived a solitary existence in a house in Virginia Street, just behind his refinery premises, and was already in his forties when he married a girl twenty five years his junior. When he and his family took up residence at Avery Hill, Boyd was already fifty seven and the eldest of his four children just ten years old.

Sir John Boyd sugar merchant 1<sup>st</sup> baronet (1718-1800) built Danson House in Danson Park his son Sir John Boyd 2<sup>nd</sup> Baronet, another sugar merchant (1750-1815) - maybe these are related to this Boyd?

*'The World – Celebrity at Home'* profile of North in 1888, suggests that Sir William Cubitt had been commissioned to build Avery Hill twenty five years previously, but he was more a civil engineer than a builder of houses, and it could refer to his namesake another unrelated William Cubitt, but even he, as the builder of Covent Garden Market and Fishmonger's Hall, would probably have been above such a modest undertaking as Avery Hill. Incidentally, a Thomas Cubitt built the Grosvenor Estate for the Duke of Westminster.

A number of individual farms were combined to create the estate of Avery Hill. Boyd was responsible for developing the parkland and planted most of the fine specimen trees many of which are still to be found at Avery Hill. When North took up residence in 1883, Avery Hill was already a house of impressive proportions, but altogether too modest for our Colonel, who on his return from Chile having made a fortune, was poised to make his entry into society. North, developed the Winter Garden, the Italianate Garden and much of the parkland as you see it today. Colonel North's death notice in the New York Times (6.4.1896) reported; *"Colonel North had a mansion in the outskirts of Eltham, in Kent, which was sumptuous and hospitable. Avery Hill is as celebrated in England as Walpole's Strawberry Hill was."*

Sadly this is no longer true, as even many Eltham residents (myself included, until I embarked on this account) are unaware of the existence of the remains of the Colonel's fine house.

# Chapter One

## Early Days; Leeds 1842-1869

John Thomas North was born on 30th Jan 1842 at number 7 Bywater Street, a narrow road of back-to-back houses in Holbeck, a suburb of Leeds. This was an area of railway sidings and huge foundries belching out smoke – which conjures up images of William Blake's 'dark satanic mills'. His father was a coal merchant and local churchwarden as well as being active in the local Conservative party. John Thomas was the second of four children born to James and Mary North (née Gambles). Emma the eldest child had been born in 1839, Harry in 1845 and third son Gamble in 1854. This was the height of the Industrial Revolution and Holbeck was at the epicentre, with its foundries and mills manufacturing machinery, some of which was exported both nationally and internationally. So it was entirely fitting that elder son John should be destined to be an engineer, and also perhaps explains his later trans-Atlantic ventures. The 1851 census has the family living at 6 Salem Place in Hunslet with JTN described as scholar aged 9. The young John Thomas wouldn't have had far to go to school and church, as the Salem School and Salem Chapel stood side-by-side in Salem Place.

Image 1; No 7 Bywater St (1st house) 1959

essential to Britain's progress during the Industrial Revolution, of which the north of England was the powerhouse. It is ironic that government today continue to talk of creating a new *Northern Powerhouse* almost two centuries later – the north of England having lost much of it's industrial predominance by the mid- 20<sup>th</sup> century.

John Thomas had left school aged fifteen to be apprenticed to the company of millwrights and shipwrights, Shaw, North and Watson of Hunslet, Leeds – this North seems to have been a cousin of his father's and in 1865, having served his eight-year apprenticeship, North joined the larger firm of *Fowler and Company* at their *Steam Plough Works*, also in Hunslet, which with the spread of railways and the coming of steam locomotives, became the *Steam Plough and Locomotive Works*. Robert Fowler took over the running of the company following the premature death of his brother John in 1864 and went on to become a personal friend of North's and subsequently had some involvement in the London nitrate *scene*.

North had assumed a position of some responsibility at Fowlers - he was now a foreman on 12s a week but not yet in a position to ask for the hand of the young lady he had been seeing, Jane Woodhead. Jane was the daughter of local painter/plumber/glazier, and senior Conservative and Leeds Town Councillor, John Woodhead of 61, Park Lane. There is an amusing account in the Woolwich Gazette of 2nd Sep 1887, where North recounts his *courtship* of Jane thus:-

> *'Wages were eighteen shillings I was in love with a girl who was working at a neighbouring factory in Hunslet, Leeds. We'd had many a talk about getting married, but when I was only getting twelve shillings a week, and she was only getting eight, we came to the conclusion that it wouldn't do. I said, 'My lass, ahm rayht fond o tha, and the moment I get a rise in screw we'll risk it, and we'll face the world, lass, for good or for ill.' She gave me a hug and kissed me, and from that day to this she's been my best adviser, friend, and comforter.'*

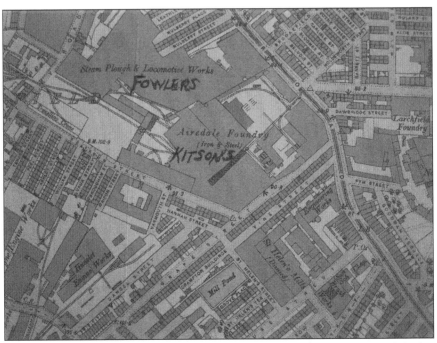

Image 2; Leeds (Hunslet) 1890

John Thomas North and Jane Woodhead married on August 8th 1866 and they are both shown as being 24 on the marriage certificate. Jane was probably quite relieved that they could finally afford to get married, as at 24 and unmarried she may have felt she was destined to become an *old maid!* Judging from North's comments quoted above, theirs seems to have been a good partnership, as in those patriarchal times, it would have been unusual for a Victorian husband to have considered their wife, their *best adviser.*

It was reported that in typical generosity of spirit, John Thomas had relinquished his part of the inheritance on his father's death, in his mother's favour. John Thomas and Jane's first-born Harry, had arrived in 1866, with daughter Emma following in 1868. The third and last child Arthur Jewell was something of a postscript arriving as he did fifteen years later in 1883 when North had returned from his spell in Chile.

# Chapter Two

## Peru 1869; The Adventure Begins; Nitrate

There are conflicting accounts as to what exactly took North to Peru and his exact year of setting off, but by the time his second child Emma was born in 1868, it seems he must have been preparing to undertake the arduous trans-Atlantic journey to South America. It is a measure of North's pioneer and risk-taking spirit that he should contemplate such an epic journey to the other side of the world, when most of his Leeds contemporaries would be unlikely to venture further than the nearest town in their lifetimes. This journey would have been a daunting prospect at any time, let alone with a wife and two small children in tow. Steamships had by this time reduced the Atlantic crossing from around seven weeks to 10 days but we cannot know for sure whether North and his family took the steam route at £6 per head or the longer/cheaper £3 per head sailing – I suspect he would have taken the steamer as he was going as a representative of Fowlers who would probably have wanted to get their man installed as soon as possible. Whichever it was, it would have been a momentous undertaking and with the opening of the Panama Canal still being thirty years away, the journey would have necessitated a negotiation of the treacherous Cape Horn as Peru was on the west coast of South America.

On these crossings, there would be just a deck separating the better-off passengers like the North's from the many poorer immigrants crammed into the hold who were also setting out in the hope of finding a better life – rich or poor these travellers faced the same dangers on this still dangerous crossing (remember Titanic is still almost 50 years away!). The transportation of immigrants was the main source of income for the operators of these trans-Atlantic ships. Disease was always a danger on these long crossings, especially with so many people crammed in close quarters with an outbreak of cholera or typhus being ever-present. The North's probably had slightly better food and more comfortable accommodation but all were sharing the same the same perils of those who cross the sea.

More than one account says North was happy to go as he already had a brother in South America - Edmundson mentions a tombstone of a Harry North (died aged 38 in 1883) in a Tiliviche cemetery in the nitrate region of Chile. North himself gave various conflicting accounts as to his reasons for going to South America; in '*Col. North How He Made His Millions*', North states he '*seized the chance to better myself*', offering to go for his usual wages of 18s per week, even offering to cover his own expenses. In his triumphal return visit to Chile in 1889, he describes a stop at Carrizal Bajo, a port some twenty miles from Huasco, where North pointed out to the assembled party a building which had been the workshop where he had first toiled '*driving rivets into boiler iron for four dollars a day*' – at around five American dollars to the £ at the time, this is already a vast improvement on his 18s a week in Leeds. Some claim he was sent by Fowler's '*to set up some nitrate equipment*' in 1867, while Harold Blakemore in '*British Nitrates and Chilean Politics 1886 -1896 Balmaceda and North*' published 1974, states that Fowlers sent North to South America in 1866-67 to supervise construction of locomotives on the Carrizal railway, while yet another account has North being sent to a copper-mining zone near Caldera. However, in his earlier article for History Today '*John Thomas North, the Nitrate King*' published 1962, Blakemore states that North '*first went to Peru in*

*1869 when the engineering firm of Fowler & Company, sent him out to set up machinery for the extract of nitrate'* and this seems to be the likeliest scenario for North setting out aged 27, with his wife, small son Harry and baby daughter Emma, for Tarapaća on the west coast of Peru. I will just add here that North arrived in Peru in 1869 but this same region became part of Chile, as did all of Bolivia's coastline following the War of the Pacific in 1879.

By his own account, he arrived in the New World with £10 in his pocket, but given that North himself liked to weave those *'rags to riches'* stories and newspapers propensity to perpetuate those myths, it is difficult to separate fact from fiction. What is apparent is that by any account, North was both a risk-taker and adventurer in undertaking such a journey at all. He was crossing the globe to a most inhospitable desert region that did not even have a proper water supply, as Alfred Jeffrey said in his 1984 letter that I read amongst the UOG archive. Jeffrey says, men such as North were subsequently vilified as *plunderers,* but had it not been for their doggedness and pioneering spirit there would have been no nitrate industry in Chile and therefore no source of tax revenues for the Chilean government.

### *The Nitrate*

The whole question of what exactly constituted nitrate proved a difficult one for me to establish. Many accounts still claim that North made his money in guano when it was in fact *sodium nitrate* or *nitrate of soda,* as it was sometimes called, that built his fortune. There were various nitrate compounds resulting in, amongst other things, either explosives or fertilisers. Indeed an article in the Dartford Express of 1888, when trying to explain the origin of the North fortune states:-

> *'Your own ideas concerning the nature of nitrate are hopelessly confused by a vague notion that it has something to do with fireworks, photography or a specific for influenza. But an Eltham schoolboy could probably inform you with praiseworthy*

*promptitude, that the chemical equivalent of nitrate of soda is NaNO3; that it is the great fertiliser of the near future.'*

Mixing nitrate, potash, and phosphoric acid results in a powerful fertiliser. Mix nitrate with charcoal and sulfur, the result is explosive black powder.

*To summarise:- potassium nitrate (KNO3 'K' being Potassium) results in gunpowder – while sodium nitrate (NaNO3 'Na' being Sodium) results in fertiliser.*

In a Guardian article of 2nd June 2014 entitled *'Caliche: the conflict mineral',* Daniel Gross writes:-

'Nitrates are a stable and usable form of the nitrogen found in our atmosphere, and they feed two of mankind's oldest activities: agriculture and war. If you mix nitrates, potash, and phosphoric acid into soil, crops grow with a new vitality. If you mix them with charcoal and sulfur, the result is explosive black powder. Nitrates dissolve easily, however, and almost never accumulate in nature. Back in the 1830s, desert nitrates still competed with nitrate-rich guano deposits, but as guano supplies dwindled, the South American desert became the world's last remaining viable source. A swelling stream of miners in search of "white gold" began to settle the desert.'

I am surprised he did not mention North, who after all was the main mover in the booming nitrate industry in the 19th century.

As already stated, some accounts claim that the Colonel's fortune had been made in *guano,* but I already knew that North's nitrate was not bird-droppings that were harvested from the cliffs, but was open-cast mined and then put through some chemical process. My chemical/ scientific knowledge is rudimentary, but I had been able to ascertain that much. What also proved confusing was the fact that North went to Peru as that was where the nitrate regions were, but due to *The War of the Pacific*, Chile as the victor, moved her border northwards taking in the nitrate regions of both Peru and Bolivia. So having gone to Peru, North subsequently returned from the same region, but it was now part of Chile.

While there are some claims that the indigenous Indian tribes had long known of the fertilising powers within this *White Gold*, there is no evidence to support this and up until the first quarter of the 18th century, the outside world was ignorant of its uses. And so, fortuitously, North arrives in South America just as a *White Gold* rush was about to take off

By the 1870's, Nitrate was already taking over as a viable alternative to guano, found mostly on the Peruvian Chincha Isles, which by this time were almost depleted. The only significant deposits of sodium nitrate were to be found in the desert region of what is now northern Chile (Peru/Bolivia pre 1883), in a rectangular coastal strip, roughly 15 miles by 350 miles. Around the beginning of the nineteenth century a Scotsman living near the port town of Iquique, near the Atacama Desert and at the time part of Peru, is credited with having first discovered the fertilizing powers of nitrate after noticing how much his crop flourished once he had spread some of this native soil containing *white crystals* on it. Soil samples were sent back to Scotland for analysis and the amazing fertilizing powers of nitrate were confirmed. However, it was only after the European discovery of a formula for the conversion of the unrefined nitrate-bearing rock into usable sodium nitrate that large-scale production was possible with the end product being exported via boat to Lima, capital of Peru and thence on to North America and Europe. The fertilizing power of sodium nitrate helped fuel the huge world expansion in agriculture at the time and a burgeoning nitrate industry in Peru/Bolivia/Chile. Although our atmosphere is four-fifths nitrogen, it is only through the soil that plants draw their source, which is then passed to animals through the plants. It is ironic that while being a powerful fertilizer, nitrate was of itself, unable to support life, hence its location in the desert regions. Nitrate was also an ingredient in the manufacture of explosives, until the First World War saw its replacement with a synthetic substitute.

Again from the Guardian article of 2014, discussing the impact of nitrate during the First World War:-

'The allies may have had Chile's nitrates at their disposal, but the central powers had chemistry. As many historians have argued, the war dragged on largely because German scientists, particularly <u>Fritz Haber and Carl Bosch</u>, managed to match the Allied supply by <u>synthesising nitrates</u> on an industrial scale. What is still up for debate is whether Germany's losses in Chile were a strategic failure, putting the country at great risk of losing the war, or instead a shrewd calculation based on knowledge of the impending Haber-Bosch process.'

Harold Blakemore's article *'John Thomas North, the Nitrate King'*, published in History Today in the 1960's, claims that the development of the nitrate industry was *'fertilised by British capital'*. Indeed, the nitrate trade, quickly became dominated by the British, who at this time were in the midst of the Industrial Revolution. By 1820, there were already at least twelve British nitrate firms established in the Chilean port of Valparaiso and by 1860, 2,000 British subjects, half the total for the whole country, were resident there. This was essentially an English colony, with English as the dominant language and trade conducted in pounds sterling – they even had their own newspaper *The Chilean Times* – so it seems the young North family joined an already well established British community with many names such as Edwards, Ross and Blest amongst the great Anglo-Chilean families from the beginning of the 19th century. 1830 had seen the first shipment of nitrate to Europe where it was rapidly taken up by farmers eager to maximise crop yields. German and French farmers were most keen on nitrate, British farmers less so, maybe be expected their fertilisers to be brown and smell foul, whereas nitrate was pure white and odourless.

The following account I have taken from Jay Sivell's blog of his ancestor Bert's experience as a sailor on a nitrate-transporting vessel, the square-rigger *Monkbarns,* on a round-trip to Chile in 1912:-

'The nitrate trade was one of the last in which sailing ships could compete against steam. Sailing ships did not rely on expensive supplies of coals and water and so could afford to hang about beyond the sand bars for months while an awkward cargo was ferried out to them slowly, boat by boat. Guano was worse, a throat-catching green powder of ancient bird droppings shovelled off rocky outcrops further north, off Peru, and stowed in the holds by men who could only work 20 minutes at a time before they choked. The crews of guano ships were known to flee into the rigging to escape the ammoniac fumes. But the nitrate was in many respects no better.

Nitrate was white, mined and stewed in the distant desert where no rain falls from one year to the next and until the railways came, carried to the sea by pack mules that died of thirst along the way. It had to be stowed dry. But out in the anchorages, in the holds lifting and falling in the long Pacific swell, the evaporation from the bags was known to kill rats and even woodlice, and ships' cats who curled up on the sacks in dark corners grew lethargic and died.

Monkbarns had dropped anchor in Caleta Buena, north of Iquique, the smallest and bleakest of the nitrate ports, clinging to the edge of the Tarapaca desert. "We have fallen into a lovely hole this time and no mistake," wrote Bert.

A hand-tinted postcard shows a shore line of sheds cowering beneath what looks like an 8,000ft slag heap, slashed by a mountain railway like an appendix scar — "practically all there is to be seen here". Out in the bay the ships rolled at anchor in the heave of the Pacific "just as if they were at sea". They were there for over a month, with nothing to look at but railway sidings and spindly jetties.

All hands discharged their Australian coal and heaved the nitrate – nowadays considered dangerous to actually handle — bag by bag down the hatches for two months. Bert sent postcard views of the exposed bay, the long jetties battered by the breakers, and the cross-hatch of distant roofs and railway lines that petered out into rubble tracks up into the surrounding mountains. Thirty or forty ships heaved and rolled with the swell in lines beyond the surf, as restless as if they were in the open sea.'[2]

Nitrate mining, when compared to other mining industries, had relatively low operational costs but generated high profits. However, until the mid-19th century, exploitation of this resource was on a small scale with ventures frequently failing in the harsh desert climate and also from want of investment. The population of Chile by this time, was two-thirds *mestizo* ,or mixed-race, many of the European settlers having inter-married with the indigenous Indian population which had been decimated due to the introduction of European diseases like measles to which they had no immunity.

The nitrate industry in both Peruvian Tarapaća and Bolivian Antofagasta was run mainly by Chileans and British, with most of the population of these coastal regions being Chilean, which became a concern to both the Peruvian and Bolivian governments and a contributing factor in *The War of the Pacific*. The Chilean Census of 1875 shows 15.000 Chileans living in Peruvian Tarapaća and 4,800 in Bolivian Antofagasta. Nitrate became Chile's chief export and many poorer Chilean agricultural workers were attracted by the higher pay. Populations clustered around the nitrate-rich regions and ports, while many thousands of square miles remained without a single living thing. The Spanish *conquistadores* had introduced a land tenure system that resulted in a small land-owning class and a large landless peasant-class. These subsistence farmers would have been used to hard work but conditions in the nitrate fields were back-breaking, their day lasting from sunrise to sunset sometimes in 40c heat. Many nitrate areas had not seen rain for a decade, others

2   https://monkbarns.wordpress.com/2010/06/17/a-sailors-life

were lucky if it rained for a few minutes in the year and Dr Tower (see below), postulates *'if absolute desert exists in the world, it lies in the nitrate pampa'*.

While accessing the UOG archives, I came across a very poignant letter written in April 1984 by one Alfred Edmund Jeffrey who was born in Chile in 1904 and whose father was a contemporary of North's there. He tells us that North was known as *El Gringo* and *Water God* by the native Aymara and Quechua people. He tells of *foreigners*, British predominantly, trying to develop a desert region which had lain desolate through lack of water until investment, both physical and financial from those who employed their skills, expertise and capital, to discover sources of water that might support life there. These pioneers were then dubbed *Colonists* by their less-adventurous brethren who chose to stay at home. Jeffrey goes on to say that he wants to publish his book '*The Fair Gods Across the Waters*' before he dies, he is 80 at this point. He is semi-literate he confesses, not having read a book until he was eleven, living as they did in the awful *Desert of Atacama* – the *Land of the Dead*, as it was known in Inca history. North was a family friend when they were in Iquique and Jeffrey's family continued to operate one of the last few nitrate of soda mines left, up until the early 1980's. I can only assume that this gentleman was unsuccessful in his hopes of publishing, as I cannot find any reference to this book, which is a shame as it was sure to have made interesting reading.

Wages in the *oficinas* were paid in *fichas* (tokens) issued by the plant and only redeemable for goods at the issuing office, therefore giving unscrupulous plant owners a monopoly in the supply of essentials to their workforce, which many abused. These tokens had been justified due to the lack of available currency and the possibility of robbery but had been ruled illegal in 1852 in Peru, however, many British nitrate companies continued to use them. In '*A Visit to Chile…*', Russell defends these shops and the use of the *fichas, because without them the men would be left without the basic necessities, having drunk and gambled their wages.* With the *fichas* they were able to purchase essentials with the money then being deducted from their wages.

The nitrate region was known as one of the most inhospitable places on Earth. In 1913 an American geologist Dr. Walter Tower wrote:-

'In crossing this region one cannot help feeling the utter helplessness of man in the face of such great expanses of waterless and lifeless wastes ... One fails at first to understand how men are willing to live there year after year.'

This was a question that I had asked myself early on in my research as to North's motivation for such a seemingly fraught undertaking.

Dr. Tower ventures an answer;-

> *'But almost the first day's stay reveals part of the reason. The day is not unpleasant despite the heat and the intensity of the sunlight, for the extreme dryness makes temperatures of 90° or more quite comfortable, and the colors—the grays, yellows, violet—playing over the sands, help make up for the lack of living green. The nights are wonderful—cool, crisp, refreshing, with the brilliancy of sky that only deserts can have; while the moonlight gleaming from millions of salt crystals lights up the land with an effect of half day and renders into attractive forms the most prosaic objects.'*

He goes on to mention North (but not by name!):-

'To get water for the maquinas (nitrate plants?) is not everywhere easy, for the water supply always has been the chief problem in this region. Seacoast towns for a long time depended on supplies brought by vessels from four or five hundred miles farther south. It is interesting to note here that one of the prominent figures in the development of the industry after 1880 was an English iron worker, who is said to have come out to Chile to work on the tanks or boilers of some of these water-carrying vessels, and who later went home a 'nitrate millionaire'.

Large oficinas, with their many hands and their families, may make communities of 2,000 to 3,000 persons. Schools are provided by the government, the teachers getting 150 pesos to 200 pesos per month, to which some companies add 100 pesos or more, in addition to the customary free quarters, heat and water. Priests and physicians make regular visits. Musical and social clubs are organized; bands give open-air concerts two or three times a week, and worse music may be heard in many more favored parts of the world. Football is a favorite sport and there is keen rivalry between teams representing neighboring oficinas. There is the inevitable biograph (biographical sketch), a dance hall, annual visits by a circus, a saloon and even a gambling house, for since the men will gamble anyway, it is deemed best to have it done where some control may be exerted over it. Little trouble ever arises, for the resident manager is in some ways a local czar, with the very efficient mounted police of the pampa to assist in keeping order

But in the bright sun and dry air of the desert, most disease germs do not thrive, and there filth, unpleasant as it may be, does not lead to the sickness which it might cause elsewhere.'[3]

So in many ways it would seem that life in the desert was possibly healthier than that in the damp climate of England where respiratory illness was rife.

The Sep 1888 'Celebrity at Home' profile of Colonel North, mentions the Iquique Jockey Club, so life must have been quite bearable for those like the North's, who were at the higher end of the social spectrum. And, while life in the nitrate fields was undoubtedly hard, it must not be forgotten that it was just as hard, if not harder for miners back in Britain, at this time.

---

3    Popular Science Monthly Sep 1913 'The Nitrate Fields of Chile' Dr Walter Tower University of Chicago

There were already on-going border disputes between Chile and Bolivia, concerning access to nitrate deposits. In 1825, the Atacama region, where most deposits were centred, was in Bolivian territory. Peru became involved in the build-up to war, when it used its naval power

COLONEL JOHN T. NORTH, THE NITRATE KING.—[See Page 142.]

Image 3; North in Native Dress

to assist Bolivia in her own border dispute with Chile. Peru and Bolivia had made a secret pact for mutual support in their disagreements with Chile. Next crisis came in 1878 when Bolivia sought to levy a tax on Chilean-British nitrate extraction.

In the subsequent War of the Pacific 1879-1883, involving Peru, Chile and Bolivia, the Peruvian government was determined to take the nitrate industry into state ownership. However by 1882, the Peruvian nitrate fields were under the jurisdiction of victorious Chile whose government then decided to return the deposits to the private ownership of those individuals (including North) to whom bonds had been issued by the Chilean authorities. Nitrate was dubbed *White Gold* for good reason - on his return to England in 1882, North became a catalyst for a nitrate boom on the London Stock Exchange, with British investments, especially those companies established by North, coming to dominate the industry through the use of joint stock companies.

My research yielded an interesting article from the South Wales Daily News of 4th Aug 1892 asking:-

> *'Can't we produce our own nitrate of soda instead of being dependent upon South America?'*

The author suggests nitrogen-rich crop rotation would achieve this (early organic thinking). He hopes that *'We may some day grow our own nitrogen far cheaper than we can buy it from Colonel North'*. But of course North had diversified his investments away from nitrates, long before a synthetic substitute had been invented. This made me wonder how Chile responded to the prospect of the Europeans being able to synthetically produce nitrate, and then I remembered Nitrato de Chile posters in La Palma in the Canary Islands while on holiday (see Additional Information).

So when North arrived in Peru, British companies were already well established in the nitrate industry there and he was considered a bit of a '*Johnny come lately*'. By 1871 he had left Fowlers and moved up to Iquique, a port in the province of Tarapaća in southern Peru and a centre for the emerging nitrate industry. Here, the 29 year-old North went to work at the Santa Rita nitrate processing plant belonging to a Peruvian, Jose Maria Gonzalez Velez, probably initially as a boilermaker processing the raw sodium nitrate, eventually progressing to the position of chief engineer. Velez would have been aware of North's reputation as an engineer and seems to have left him to his own devices.[4] He was now well placed to gain first-hand knowledge of the workings of the nitrate trade and the prospects that industry presented to an enterprising young man like himself especially with his mechanical/industrial engineering background. He was quick to recognise the central importance of machinery and the availability of basic provisions, especially water, to the effective and productive operating of the *oficinas* (processing plants).

---

4    Osgood Hardy 1948

# Chapter Three

## 1870-1882 Building the Empire

In Iquique, surrounded as it was by desert, the water that was essential to both the running of the machines and the sustenance of those who operated them was understandably at a premium in a region that may not have seen rain for a decade. This necessity now presented itself as the first business opportunity to the enterprising and ingenious mind of North *the engineer*. By 1875, he found himself in a position to buy a rusty old steamer and kit it out as a water tanker using his engineering ingenuity. The hold would have been divided into tanks with pumps fitted for the rapid loading/unloading of water. This vessel then operated out of the port of Huanillos, plying the coast just south of Iquique. The added speed gained from newly-discovered steam power meant he could easily outpace the competition in their antiquated sailboats. Mrs North seems to have been hands-on in this business, helping her husband by taking orders and collecting payment from customers. To do this, she employed local people who drove carts from house to house filling buckets and bottles with the precious commodity. North would claim later that his water business had been exceptionally profitable.

Image 4; Liverpool Nitrate Co, Oficina

Image 5; Men Working Primitiva Nitrate Fields

North's wheeler-dealer attributes now come into their own as he manages to secure a government contract for the supply of drinking water to the whole province. He ingeniously devised a condensation system for de-salination of the salt water. Other businessmen, impressed by North's enterprise came forward as backers and enabled the rapid expansion of the business. He now went further and devised a system of floating reservoirs which meant he had all the necessary infrastructure in place once he acquired a contract from 'Guillermo' Speedie to work the Porvenir nitrate field and processing plant.

Although now having a foothold in the nitrate industry, it was really the *War of the Pacific* which provided North with the opportunity to purchase large tranches of bonds in the Peruvian nitrate industry, which subsequently laid the foundations to his becoming one of the richest men in the world within less than a decade.

The *War of the Pacific* (1879-83) was pursued between Bolivia, Peru and Chile and could be seen as essentially about national boundaries and their significance to the nitrate deposits and the tax received therefrom. Early nitrate extraction had begun in the 1860's in Bolivia but financed by a group of Chilean/British investors and at the outbreak of the war this group had interests in both Peruvian Tarapaća and Bolivian Antofagasta. Peru was alarmed at the number of Chileans involved in the nitrates industry on their territories. They had already defaulted on their national debt in 1876 and this had particularly affected British and French bondholders.

As victor at the end of the war, Chile pushed its border 400 miles northward, annexing the nitrate-rich regions of both Peru and Bolivia, with Bolivia losing all its coastline in the process. When Chile annexed Iquique and the surrounding province of Tarapacá from Peru, the Chilean government transferred ownership of the nitrate fields to the bondholders, of whom North was predominant. North was thus able to take a monopoly share of the lucrative Chilean nitrate industry for a very small initial investment, becoming known as *The King of Nitrates* in the process. The lucrative nitrate regions of both Peru (Pisagua, Iquique, Tarapaća) and Bolivia (Antofagasta) and the Atacama Desert that spanned all three countries, were now Chilean territory.

North built upon his nitrates business by expanding into further monopolies in waterworks and freight railways, while also owning several iron and coal fields. He maintained his monopolies by employing lawyers to block competing entrepreneurs both in court and within the Chilean National Congress. This was tolerated by Chilean president Domingo Santa María, but Santa María's successor, José Manuel Balmaceda, became concerned that Tarapacá was starting to resemble a *state within a state* and resolved to break North's monopoly. Balmaceda had to force competition reforms through against opposition in congress, amongst a series of disputes which would eventually escalate into the 1891 *Chilean Civil War* between the president and the congress.

In 1875, in an effort to both raise cash and take control back for the national interest, Peru had nationalised the nitrate industry in the province of Tarapaća. In 1877 state certificates were issued to the owners as compensation. However, no revenue was raised and yet the certificates were never cancelled, and these were bearer bonds and therefore payable to the holder. The *War of the Pacific*, finally ended in 1883 with the Treaty of Acon ceding Peru's Tarapaća province to Chile. In the separate Treaty of Valparaiso in 1884, Bolivia relinquished her entire nitrate-rich coastline of Antofagasta to Chile. This outcome saw Chile increase its territory by a third. Many accused North of having colluded with the Chilean military by lending several boats for the transport of wounded soldiers – in fact, he had initially refused, but the boats were nevertheless commandeered with the promise of a million francs worth of guano deposits on adjacent islands, as compensation. Chile won, North had his guano and realised a handsome profit of four million francs (£160,000). North had arrived.

Lady Bountiful continued to smile on North; the English owners of the Tarapacá Waterworks Company had fled at the beginning of the war and victorious Chile magnanimously decided to recognise North (who had previously been just a customer) as their owner. North now had a valuable monopoly for the supply of water to the port. In addition, with Chile now in control of the Tarapacá nitrate fields he saw great opportunities and was lucky enough to secure the concession to work a hitherto unexplored nitrate field and thus was the foundation laid for his nitrate fortune. However, there was still the outstanding matter of the Peruvian nitrate certificates issued by the then government in 1877 – in the uncertain political climate, these were now being traded at 80-90% below face value as they were effectively, the title deeds to the underlying *oficinas*, or nitrate fields. By 1881, certificates originally worth £180 were selling at £20-30. North, through his contacts, was in a good position to assess the potential value of the underlying assets and knew that these bonds represented important pockets of nitrate. In bullish fashion, North set about acquiring as many of these bonds as he could lay his hands on as his instincts (some say insider knowledge) told him Chile would be victorious and that they would honour these bonds. This is the first of North's business transactions which drew opprobrium from hostile observers both then and now. Did he have insider knowledge of Chile's intention to honour? He certainly had the business connections to the investment funds necessary to take advantage of any opportunity that might present itself. In addition he had friends in the right places. At the outbreak of the war, his friend Robert Harvey was Inspector General of Nitrates for the Peruvian government and as such would certainly have been a source of knowledge as to any movements within the nitrate industry. His acquaintance with John Dawson, who in 1879 was manager of the Chilean Banco de Valparaiso in Iquique, meant he would have had access to the necessary funding. All the pieces of the jigsaw were in place to guarantee a favourable outcome for the *Chemical Conquistador*. Once it was known that Chile would honour the bonds, North's investment increased a hundred-fold as nitrate production which had previously been in Peruvian and Bolivian provinces, was now on Chilean soil.

In honouring the bonds, the Chileans were being pragmatic rather than generous. Marxist historians claim the Chilean government under Balmaceda wanted to nationalise the nitrate industry and was hindered in doing so by British capitalists and North in particular, but Edmundson claims there is no evidence to support this premise. In the event, the Chilean government chose this course rather than nationalise the industry and risk upsetting influential backers both Chilean and British. North thus acquired some of the richest nitrate deposits and was set to become one of the prime *movers and shakers* of the industry. History has been critical of what they saw as the Chilean government selling off *the family silver* and has characterised North as a *pantomime-baddie grasping capitalist*. The reality seems to have been, the Chilean authorities had no real alternative if they were going to kick-start the export of nitrate following the conflict and an urgent need to replenish the coffers depleted by war, with a tax on the export of nitrates. There was a mutual dependence between the Chilean economy and the mainly British investors. Chile did not have the technology or the finance to exploit the nitrate for itself and would not want to alienate those men like North on whose expertise their economy depended. These undertakings were not without an element of risk to North himself as he would still need to invest heavily in machinery for his nitrate interests.

By 1880, North's friend and business associate Robert Harvey, had switched sides to become Inspector General of Nitrates for the Chilean authorities. Some historians claim (Hernan Ramirez Necochea 1958??Publication) that Harvey abused his position for the benefit of himself and his business associates. It is said that he and North became partners with the specific aim of buying up nitrate certificate in the firm knowledge, through Harvey's government contacts, that they would indeed be honoured by the Chilean administration. With Peru faring badly in the War of the Pacific, Peruvian bondholders were eager to divest themselves of this risky asset for whatever they could get.

By 1881, European investors, mostly British, held about £30million in Peruvian nitrate certificates. They set up the *Peruvian Bondholders Committee* to ensure that the Chilean government understood their claim and the fact that it was upheld by the British government. North and Robert Harvey bought up bonds at knock-down prices, gambling on Chile honouring them, which they did in 1881, while the War of the Pacific was still ongoing, and therefore the future of the nitrate industry, as yet unsure.

1882 saw Harvey and North return to Britain in order to establish the joint stock companies with which they hoped to exploit to full effect the nitrate interests they had acquired at bargain-basement prices. North and his partners were now in control of a major portion of a global monopoly as the only significant deposits of nitrate were in Chile. North was well on his way to becoming *The Nitrate King*.

As manager of the Chilean Banco de Valparaiso, North's friend John Dawson, had been well placed to advance the necessary funding to acquire the bonds. Later, in 1888, having returned to England, North and Dawson set up the Bank of Tarapaća and London, with Robert Harvey becoming a director in 1894. Another vital business associate was Maurice Jewell and so close was their friendship, that North's second son born in Sep 1883 was almost certainly named after him as Arthur Jewell North. Jewell had been appointed British Vice Consul in Iquique, but that had not stopped him from forming a trading partnership with North to act as shipping agents and suppliers to the nitrate plants. This arrangement was not however exclusive and each partner was free to pursue any business interests outside of the remit of the North and Jewell partnership. Relations between the two families were later soured following the early death of Jewell in 1895; his executors claimed that monies were still owed to the family from the partnership. North disputed this and a law suit ensued which was only resolved after North's own premature demise 1896.

# Chapter Four

## 1882 Return to England - Nitrate Boom; dubious business practices

On his return to England in 1882, North's activities were instrumental in triggering what came to be known as the *nitrate boom*. This was achieved by utilising joint stock companies, similar to corporations, to maximise his nitrate investment returns on the London Stock Exchange. An application for membership of the *Institution of Mechanical Engineers* was made in August of that year, presumably to add professional weight to his background, giving his address as '*Cedars, East Dulwich Rd, Peckham London SE*'. In addition, he went into partnership with the existing partners of the Liverpool trading company of *William and John Lockett*, having made the acquaintance of one of the partners, John Waite, while the latter was on a business trip to Peru. Using Lockett finance, the *Liverpool Nitrate Company* was formed in 1883 with North as chairman and his friend Robert Harvey a director. Ties between the Norths and the Locketts were strong with North's daughter Emma marrying George Alexander Lockett at Holy Trinity Church Eltham in 1892, an occasion to which her father had issued invitations to several Rothschilds as well as half a dozen titled members of the plutocracy. This was another occasion for the newspapers to indulge in wild flights of fancy, some claiming that Emma had been given a dowry of '*half a million!*'.

The Ramirez nitrate plant, now owned by the Liverpool Nitrate Company, was the first of North's holdings to be exploited through a joint stock company with shares being sold to wealthy investors who provided capital but with limited risk to themselves, supposedly. Through his joint stock companies, North could be deemed responsible for the introduction of nitrates to the London Stock Exchange. The Ramirez holding had originally cost £5000 for the purchase of the underlying certificates, and was then sold to the company by North and Robert Harvey for £50,000. Meanwhile, the *Shanks* process, improving nitrate processing and maximising profits and therefore dividends, was introduced in 1878, but this system required heavy investment in new machinery. Harvey set about securing the latest machinery to equip the Ramirez plant and he returned to Iquique in 1883 to create what was to become one of the best equipped nitrate plants with all the latest technology including illumination of the work area and even the first telephone to be installed in the nitrate fields. The Liverpool Nitrate Company was a significant element of North's portfolio, paying good dividends to both himself and other shareholders:- 26% in 1885 rising to 40% in 1887. The original £5 shares were now being traded at £35 – what enviable returns when viewed from todays 0.25% interest rates!

North's endeavours with another of his joint-stock companies, the *Lagunas Nitrate Company Limited,* were less favourable. Robert Harvey and Maurice Jewell were co-directors and with some sleight-of-hand they managed to sell assets to themselves at a profit and this was not apparent to other shareholders at the time. North enthusiastically predicted handsome profits and it was understandable that less sophisticated investors would be persuaded by North's seemingly *Midas touch* – he was like a pied-piper; others followed unquestioning where he led, so reassuring was he to those around him. A.M. Binstead in 'Pitcher in Paradise' 1903 Sand and Company, subtitled 'some random reminiscences, sporting and otherwise', has the following drily amusing account of North and the difficulties presented to those seeking an audience, of getting through his cordon of hangers-on:-

*'And poor old North, what a royal rough diamond was he! And what a potent and alluring come-on to the inventor on the look-out for capital, the Queen Victoria Street promoter with the wild-cat scheme, the impecunious holder of the snide 'option' on a claim in Burmah on which rubies had been found in such quantities as to menace local agriculture! To waylay the Colonel was the chief care of many a busted genius who still perambulates the asphalt of Bucklersbury, 'rain or shine' And when at last an invitation to dine on Sunday at Eltham had been gained —for, as the intelligent foreigner long since discovered, everything in England begins with a dinner, what a temporary Theebaw did the poor scheming wretch become! How little he imagined, as he made his way to Eltham in his hurrah clothes and his brain in such a whirl that he couldn't hear the traffic, that for all the chance he would get of a quiet five minutes with the Colonel, he might have climbed a tree in Hyde Park and stayed there. But so it was. The wily Colonel never coined his cherished aphorism, 'Luck is simply the faculty of seizing passing opportunities' with the least intention of himself furnishing the opportunities; and before that Sunday's gorgeous entertainment had run to any length, the man with the draft prospectus in his pocket would make the discovery that he was only one of five-and-twenty fellows who had come down on similar errands, and not one of whom, in the parlance of the pavements, had 'any earthly'.*[5]

'The Grand Promotion Army' is the title of one of the chapters in Edmundson's book 'The Nitrate King' and this *spoof* of a Music Hall song had appeared in The Financial News of May 26 1888 as 'A Stock Exchange Ballad: The Grand Promotion Army'. This seems to capture North's blustering character, while hinting at his less than transparent business machinations – I am including just the first and last verses:-

---

5   Pitcher in Paradise Pg. 215-216

*I am Colonel North of the Horse Marines*
*I began promoting when in my teens,*
*And I rather think I'm behind the scenes*
*In the Grand Promotion Army.*

*For 'some has brains and some has tin',*
*As Orton remarked; and if you'd win,*
*Why, stick to the Colonel, and all stand in*
*With the Grand Promotion Army.*

*The Nitrate King*, as North came to be known in the British press, was portrayed by them as a promotion artist who used sometimes dubious methods, in manipulating the price of stock in Chile's most valuable natural resource, for the benefit of himself and his backers. Although, undoubtedly, many of North's investors lost money, as so many did in the numerous 19th century *get-rich-quick* investment schemes, this could possibly be seen as attributable to fluctuations in nitrate demand rather than any sharp practice by North himself. Many Chilean historians, and several left-wing ones, see him as a *robber baron*, who stripped Chile of its wealth, but current reappraisals see it slightly differently, acknowledging the fact that North's position had not been without risk and that he had invested in and modernised the nitrate industry.

In *'British Nitrates and Chilean Politics 1886 -1896 Balmaceda and North'* published 1974, Harold Blakemore states that demand for nitrates in Europe had grown substantially especially from the sugar-beet fields (beet having taken over from cane) of Germany and France. Understandably, nitrate shares were in great demand on the London Stock Exchange, and chief amongst those promoting these, was of course John Thomas North. Blakemore asserts:-

*'It was his dynamic personality, business capacity and brilliant example that captivated investors. Even those who had their suspicions of North's business methods, could not deny his impact'*

Blakemore makes the claim that the real basis for North's fortune was speculative rather than any underlying company's success. I have to disagree, as had North not spent 12 years in the harsh conditions of the nitrate deserts of Chile perfecting his craft, he would not have been in a position to inspire confidence in his investors. Blakemore also presents a novel description of North as a:-

> 'celebrity who used his position as a self-made man and his popularity in the newspapers to impress the public and show an example of how to make money and what could be done with it'

North he tells us:-

> 'was a born actor and consummate showman, dazzling with his ostentation and his projection of a public image to inspire confidence in his promotions, was really the key factor in his success'

While being the darling of some newspapers, amongst them, the Financial Times, others, like The Economist, with its traditional scepticism about 'investment booms, blind capital....and all other kinds of doubtful promotion and speculation', were to be a constant source of irritation to North by the late 1880's.

North's companies continued to pay high dividends to shareholders throughout the *boom* years of nitrate and through cartels, he attempted to push up the price of his investment vehicles in a way that has been mirrored in our own time by the *tech* and *dot com* bubbles. J.Fred Rippy's 1959 '*British Investments in Latin America 1822-1949*', notes that between 1888-96 North's companies paid dividends of 306% for the Liverpool Nitrate Company, the Nitrate Railways Company 174% and the Lagunas Syndicate 100%.[6] Such was the confidence in North's business prowess that it was said in 1888 '*put North's name on a costermonger's cart, turn it into a limited liability company and the shares will be selling at 300% premium before they are an hour old*'.

---

6    J.Fred Rippy 'British Investments in Latin America 1822-1949' Univ. of Minnesota 1959

Money was to be made, but usually at the expense of the ordinary investing public on the bottom ladder of the financial *food chain*. By the time he died in 1896, North's reputation had become somewhat tarnished by what were seen as decidedly dubious stock-market machinations. The Economist in Nov 1895 reported *'grossly exaggerated estimates which induced foolish investors to buy shares at nearly 700% premium',* with the Colonel supposedly advising *'buy and hold'* while he himself was quietly off-loading those same shares.

North came to be resented also by other British nitrate companies, particularly for the monopoly in transportation he came to have through his railways, therefore affecting their own output and profits. Many felt that the nitrate *boom* owed more to North's personality and behind the scenes manipulations, than any strength in the underlying assets. Again, The Economist of Aug 3rd 1889 states *'It is seldom that the movements of one individual have such important consequences to the stocks comprising the nitrate group. The market for nitrates is essentially a one-man market'.* The article goes on to claim that a recent drop in prices was due to Col. North being away in Chile surveying his empire, the market faltering for want of the Colonel's steady grip on the tiller.

It is very probable that all this stress (a concept unknown at the time) contributed to North's early death at age 54 in 1896. Following his death, many newspapers were quick to *stick the knife in*, with The New York Times headlining *'Col. North Denounced'* in August 1896 adding *'His treatment of Shareholders Declared Little Better Than Robbery'* and that he *'was fortunate in dying when he did'.* Not exactly a eulogy.

By this time the financial press must have felt they had the measure of the Colonel and he would have been conscious of them continuously breathing down his neck. The Economist was again especially scathing, in 1894 they declared *'It is our duty to draw attention to what has taken place under Colonel North's auspices before, and to remind investors that they have no sort of guarantee that a similar catastrophe may not take place again'* - they were referring to the collapse in the nitrate industry five years previously.

Another North vehicle, *The Lagunas Nitrate Company*, turned out to be less than a success story for the ordinary investors drawn in by the Colonel's PR machine. The firm of W & J Lockett (daughter Emma's in-laws) were aggrieved enough to take legal action in 1898 (after North's death) and the courts found in their favour. This must have been a terrible time for Emma, North's daughter and now a Lockett, seeing her father's character sullied in both the press and the courts, and this following his totally unexpected death aged just 54.

North's *Primitiva Company* was another that had bad outcomes for investors. North had done the usual blustering confidence PR job to beguile investors into buying shares at an almost 700% mark-up. He talked-up the company's prospects but this became increasingly difficult as the actual results continued to disappoint. He had even offered, at a particularly heated shareholder meeting, to buy any of their shares at one and a half times current market value. This managed to keep things quiet for a while but North was having to resort to increasingly desperate measures to maintain investor confidence in his business. The Economist once more pointed out that this company which had once been valued at £1.5 million, was now, by North's own admission worth just £20,000. This was the company that he had been advising investors to *buy and hold* while quietly unloading his own shares - to other family members he later claimed.

While being lambasted in the financial press, and bogged down in various law-suits, North (contrary to press opinion) continued to invest heavily in nitrate, while also diversifying into peripheral areas such as railways, coal, water, banking and steamships. In 1887 North had bought a majority interest in the *Nitrate Railways Company* which gave him a virtual railway monopoly in the Tarapaća region, a situation that brought North into conflict with Chilean President Balmaceda and was according to many *leftist* historians, one of the contributing factors to the Civil War in 1891. High tariffs on the *Nitrate Railways,* which linked the *oficinas* of Tarapacá with the ports of Iquique and Pisagua, caused hostility amongst other produces like the Gibbs', another British nitrate company, as well as the Chilean government.

The Montero Brothers had in 1868 and 1869, been given Peruvian government approved concessions for the building of two railway lines; one linking to the Iquique nitrate fields, the other the Pisagua deposits. A third concession in 1871, and exclusive for 25 years, was for a railway to the Bolivian border, but this was never started. By 1874 the Montero Brothers had transferred most of their rights to the *National Nitrate Railways Company* in Peru, while still retaining a large proportion of the shares themselves. Company difficulties led to the formation of a new company, the *Nitrate Railways Company*, a joint-stock company registered in London in 1882 with the sole intention of acquiring the *National Nitrate Railways Company of Peru*. By 1887, North already had a controlling interest in this company – he had taken advantage of the difficulties the Montero Brothers had found themselves in, needing to raise cash in order to pay off company debt – they had instructed a London agent to raise £70,000. On applying to North, their agent was told '*I will make you an offer but it has got to be accepted or rejected by you before you leave the room. I will give you £95,000 for your interest in the railway',* - and of course the answer was a resounding '*Yes*'. Again, as with his nitrate interests, North's railway business was a continual source of conflict with the press and the government, leading to yet more litigation.

In 1886 the Chilean government moved to break the *Nitrate Railways Company's* monopoly in the Tarapacá region by cancelling the original concessions on which it was based, arguing that these were forfeited as they had been issued by the vanquished Peruvians before the War of the Pacific. More litigation ensued with North employing expensive lawyers in his attempts to lobby the Chilean Congress. President

Balmaceda prevailed and in September 1889 (after North's return from his triumphal final visit to Chile) the Council of State upheld the government's right to annul the monopoly.

It could be claimed that competing British interests, wanting to establish rival railways were also a factor in the political crisis which culminated in the Civil War of 1891. President Balmaceda's cancelling of the concessions by decree was seen as an abuse of his executive power. Balmaceda lost the Civil War but his successors were just as intent on ending the *Nitrate Railways* monopoly.

It is not unthinkable that all this stress was instrumental in North's early death as even one of his apparent robust constitution would have found the physical and mental pressure as *boom* turned to *bust*, extremely stressful.

# Chapter Five

## A Portrait of the 'King'

An article in the Dartford Express of 1st Sep 1888 which had first been published in 'The World Celebrity at Home' gives us an insightful description of the Colonel:-

*'The sun of Chili and the sands of Tarapaća have not unduly bronzed the ruddy countenance of John North; not a streak of gray is to be seen in his auburn hair and there is something essentially English in his bright-blue eyes which you can hardly help noticing.'*

Things had not changed unduly (apart from his hair going from 'not a streak of gray' to 'streaked with gray') when Harper's Weekly gave the following physical sketch of the Colonel on 6th Feb 1892:-

*'In person Colonel John Thomas North is of medium height and only moderately stout, not weighing more than 150 pounds. His hair is yellowish-red, while his whiskers and mustache (sic) are somewhat lighter and streaked with gray. His chin is shaven as in the English fashion. His complexion is ruddy, as becomes a*

*Yorkshireman, and by-the-way, though so long accustomed to speak the soft Spanish tongue, when he delivers himself in English the burr of the north of England is most conspicuous. In dress he would be called quiet were it not for his diamonds and jewelry… Such is the most conspicuous and important man owning those English interests in Chili of which we have lately heard so much.'*

*'only moderately stout'* – talk about a back-handed compliment!!

Le Figaro of Apr 23rd 1895, describing the Colonel then aged 52:

*'Most affable and sociable, strong-looking and of military appearance, very blue eyes and his hair already growing thin'*

It is a contentious point whether the Colonel spoke Spanish or not. He may not have had to communicate with his native workers directly as this would have been through his managers and foremen, however, one would have expected him to pick up a bit of the lingo

Image 6; Portrait of The King

after spending more than a decade in a Spanish-speaking country. North was often described as the quintessential *Robber Baron* and there is some truth in this. Conversely, had it not been for British skill and capital, it is unlikely that the young Chilean nation would have profited much from its own natural resources for some considerable time and Chilean Presidents other than Balmaceda recognised this. They might wish that the Chilean nation had more control of what was their main national resource but were pragmatic enough not to want to alienate British investors in the absence of Chilean ones. The ruling elite in Chile preferred to invest in mining and banking rather than industry, and so, where Chilean funds may have been employed in industrial innovation for the national good, in practice, this did not happen. Chile therefore could be said to have benefitted from the introduction of the latest technology from Britain.

*It should also be said that the infrastructure financed and built by the British remained when owners like North returned home from Chile.*

It is often claimed that North's financial machinations were less than transparent, in that profits (in dividends) were initially paid from capital derived from acquisitions sold on to companies expressly formed to exploit the assets, and enthusiastically promoted by North's ebullient personality, rather than solely from any real profit earned – it was claimed that this was essentially a Ponzi scheme, which we know are still in practice to this day, even with all our legislation regarding *transparency* in financial matters. North's business practices can be likened to an early *hedge fund manager,* as his interests seem to have been, after his return to England in 1882, more speculation and financing rather than the actual running of companies and this made him unpopular amongst those other British involved in the nitrate industry. His real talent lay in the discovery of new ways of making large amounts of money, and success will always have its detractors. However, he was recognised by the business community when granted the Freedom of the City of London on 14th November 1885.

It has already been established that there was a strong element of envy amongst North's business rivals. In '*The City of London – Vol 1 – A World of Its Own 1815-1890*', David Kynaston observes that North's rise was hugely galling to other British nitrate pioneers, like the company of Anthony Gibbs, which already had substantial interests in Chile before North's arrival, and '*had pioneered the manufacture of nitrate of soda and as London agents for the Chilean State Railway during its construction, had even been responsible for sending the young North out to Chile in the first place*' – this last claim is a moot point as it is not easy to establish beyond doubt, on whose behalf North first went to Chile. Gibbs and Company had started in London in 1808 and then opened branches in Peru and Chile in 1822, having managed to gain a contract with the Peruvian government to trade in guano. When North first arrived in Peru, Gibbs were already the senior partners in the Tarapaća Nitrate Company which was founded in 1865. It must have been hard for them to see their position eclipsed so quickly and so spectacularly, by a relative newcomer like North. Kynaston goes on to say that the Nitrate Railway was an especially sore point – with Herbert Gibbs in 1888 complaining of North '*seizing a golden opportunity, adding success to success, he has made a fortune under our very noses, in our own country, and at our own business, in which we have hardly participated at all. The result is that the gallant Colonel has completely eclipsed us in the Nitrate business and whatever he touches is dashed at by the public and driven to a premium immediately*'. The Gibbs' despair is palpable.

The Leeds Times of 5th July 1890 had the following account of a supposed chance encounter with North on a train and it could easily be fictitious, but the portrayal of the Colonel seems true to character:-

'COLONEL NORTH ON HIS WEALTH. THE NITRATE KING INTERVIEWED IN A RAILWAY CARRIAGE, OR SAID TO HAVE BEEN. A few evenings ago we (says the City Leader) had occasion to take the last train from Charing Cross to Blackheath, Whether it was that there were fewer "smoking" compartments or more smokers, we know not, but we looked in vain for a seat in which we could enjoy our Havana without fear of interruption either from the railway official or the blue ribbon army man with the asthmatical cough. Just as we were on the point of relinquishing our smoke, and were deciding to spend the journey in anathematising the railway company, we espied a familiar figure in the corner of a first-class non-smoker. IT WAS THE COLONEL, and we were saved. Surely, we thought. Colonel North will not object to the railway regulations being broken in this respect. "Do you object to smoking, Colonel?" we asked, with that familiarity which with some persons will breed contempt. "Not at all," he replied, pleasantly. "Thanks. I thought you would not." "Why?" he asked, curiously. "Well—er, you are a smoker yourself, are you not?" "I never smoke. I did once, but it rather upset me, and since that time smoking and I have not been altogether friends." Here was a surprise! The man who is always represented in his photographs as holding a cigar never smokes. Why, not long ago, according to the illustrated papers, a cigar was as inseparable from Colonel North as was that wonderful coat with the fur cuffs and collar. He looked rather surprised, though, at our next question, which was, to say the least, a rather cool one. "Does this enormous amount of wealth, Colonel, bring you a large amount of happiness in excess of other people?" "Well, it brings content—to a certain extent. "yes?" " Yes. I derive the most pleasure from assisting deserving people. Not the professional beggar, mind you, but the cases where a little help, monetary or otherwise, is really beneficial, and brings much happiness to the person assisted. Here are a number of letters of thanks which I received this morning. It gives me the greatest pleasure to read that any little assistance I may have given has been the means of helping somebody or other on in the world." 'More pleasure even than a day at Ascot? for we saw he had just come from there." "Yes, more than that even," he replied, laughingly. Then he commenced to talk about his horses and their exploits, a subject upon which he was quite at home, and we were a long way out at sea, and so we switched him off at a convenient opportunity, and asked, "Are you not bothered considerably by a lot of adventurers, who try to scrape an acquaintance with you for the purpose only of making something." " Yes, and " but we refrain from giving the remainder of the Nitrate King's reply. Though not unfit for publication, it was considerable more forceful than polite. "What do you think of Nitrates now?" "I am well satisfied with them. In the nitrate industry up till recently the production was 15 per cent, in excess of the consumption; but now the consumption is 35 per cent, in excess of the production. , "Do you use your money in the City on other things?" "No. I once tried a bit of underwriting but I made nothing out of it, and gave up the game. I never go into anything that I do not thoroughly understand." "How is the new house going along?" "Oh, very well; very well indeed." As he neared Blackheath, we summoned up enough courage to ask him if he ever condescended to glance through the forty-eight columns of the Leader. "No," he replied, with honest frankness. "Of course I have it, as I do several other financial papers; but I seldom look at any of them. The only papers I read are the Sportsman and the Sporting Life. I take a great interest in cricket. Well, good-bye. Come down and see me any Sunday you like. Good-Bye'

The chances are that this is a totally fictitious account, but it appears to contain enough of the Colonels genial character traits to make amusing reading.

The Colonel seems to have been a great patron of the Hotel Metropole, by the Strand, between Charing Cross Station and Trafalgar Square (see Additional Information), both as a temporary home for himself and his family while work proceeded on his Mansion and also as a venue for his famously lavish entertainments. In the chapter 'Millionaires at Play' in his 'Random Reminiscences' of 1911, Charles H.E. Brookfield recalls going to a midnight supper at the Café Royal (still standing by Piccadilly Circus) given by George Edwardes and attended by the Colonel, who had become so friendly with the owner/managers Charles Wyndham of the Criterion (Piccadilly) and George Edwardes of the Gaiety (Aldwych) that he gave them both an allocation of shares from one of his investment flotations. This is Brookfield's account of the evening:-

*'The guest of honour was Colonel North the Nitrate King, who was on the eve of his return trip to Chile. The Colonel arrived nearly an hour late with his secretary (not an extra-marital dalliance as secretaries tended to be male in those days), they had come straight from a City Dinner. We are told that there were several other 'industrial monarchs' present: Silver Kings and Diamond Kings, Railway Kings and Oil Kings. After a magnificent banquet, followed by music and singing, they got into private omnibuses and drove to one of the big hotels in Northumberland Avenue (Hotel Metropole). Colonel North seemed to be staying there (while renovations proceeded at Avery Hill) and we were loath to part with him. I was interested to watch millionaires at play. It was after 3am but they needed more relaxation before taking to their beds. So they got hold of the night-porter and for over half an hour they threw him sovereigns to take them, one by one, to the top of the hotel and down again in the lift. They were as eager as schoolboys. The porter must have made three or four years income in about thirty-five minutes'.*

The Colonel would have been in his element as this was exactly the sort of jolly male misbehaviour he delighted in – a sort of Victorian version of a *boys night out*. North was a member of that select band of late-Victorian self-made millionaires who delighted in entertaining each other in and around the West End and theatre-land at haunts like Romano's, Café Royal, The Ritz and The Criterion. Many of them had roughed-it for years sometimes in the world's most inhospitable places, in the accumulation of their fortunes and now they were intent on enjoying the fruits of their labours to the delight of the newspapers for whom they provided many column inches (maybe yards).

The lighter newspapers loved the Colonel and regularly printed anecdotes of the Colonel's joshing ways, whether real or imagined and these would have provided their readers with a refreshing antidote to stuffy Victorianism. Another rich source of such anecdotes is J.B.

Booth's chapter *'The Nitrate King'* in *'Palmy Days'* published in 1957, where he remembers notable characters from his days as a columnist on *The Sporting Times*. He gives a charming account of North's generosity and good spirits:-

> *'Friends frequently expostulated with the Colonel on his reckless generosity towards the group of hangers-on who perpetually sponged on him. Many of these spongers knew their man and if they were cheeky enough, maybe mentioned Yorkshire connections and made the Colonel laugh, a half-crown could be heading their way.'*

Hardly ever was an appeal for assistance made to the Colonel in vain and in most instances his gifts were spontaneous and unsolicited. Booth recounts:-

> *'One occasion at a presentation at the Midland Railway Drivers and Fireman's Life Assurance Society the Colonel on presenting compensation money to an employee as a result of injuries sustained, asked where the recipient was born 'In Leeds' came the answer. Delighted at encountering a fellow Leeds man the Colonel added another five pounds note to the sum and on further ascertaining that he was from Holbeck (North's home town) added another fiver!'*

When Edmundson describes North having entertained 300 guests at Avery Hill Picture Gallery shortly before his death, he later says this may have been the annual dinner of the Midland Railway Engine Drivers and Fireman's Assurance Society held in Birmingham on 1st May 1896 (described by Booth above).

Booth recalls another popular anecdote of the Colonel being offered a box of matches by his hostess, in order to light a cigar. After two unsuccessful attempts, his hostess noticing that he was not using the correct side of the box, suggested *'Strike it on the bottom, Colonel'* – *'A good idea!'* he exclaimed *'I didn't think of that'* and proceeded to tighten his trousers and applied the recalcitrant match with vigour!'. This again is totally fictitious for according to the man himself, he never smoked!

Just three months before his untimely death, the Colonel had attended a dinner of the Eltham Oddfellows (a mutual/friendly society forerunner to trades unions and before the Welfare State) on Feb 13th 1896, as chairman. The Sidcup and District Times of May 8th 1896 carried a report of this meeting in their article *'Death of Colonel North'*. The Colonel got the festivities going with a speech in which he declared *'I have enjoyed myself thoroughly'* - words which would shortly be enscribed on his tomb as they make a most fitting epitaph. This seems to have been a raucous evening, with much drinking, followed by cheers of *'For he's a jolly good fellow'*. Emboldened by such flattery, the Colonel had to agree that he was indeed *'a jolly good fellow'*. Our Colonel seems to have enjoyed nothing better than entertaining or being entertained and positively delighted in the camaraderie of his fellow man, in an age when it was considered natural for men to enjoy the company of other men without being considered homosexual. He was a *hail fellow, well met* sort of chap but woe betide anyone crossing him as he was quick to resort to litigation and his lawyers must have made a fortune in contesting his many lawsuits.

Again, in *'Palmy Days'*, Booth mentions Mrs. North's frustration at not knowing between twenty and thirty, how many guests to expect for any lunch or dinner. He gives an amusing account of a typical Sunday:-

*'Guests on arrival were ushered straight to the billiard room where the Colonel would already be surrounded by the early birds amongst the guests. A whisky and soda would be proffered and the wily North footmen ensured the glass remained full. Lunch with the inevitable champagne. After lunch, back to the billiard room for more whisky and soda. Among the guests was likely to*

*be John Roberts, the billiard champion, whom the Colonel would challenge, and usually beat (with a suitable handicap). Dinner, more champagne; the billiard room, more whisky and soda....'*

When Booth uses the term *guests* here, he is of course referring to *male* guests; there were of course female guests, but these would have been ushered into Mrs. North's boudoir, while their male counterparts could proceed to have a jolly good time with their host the *jolly* Colonel. And by Booth's account above, so jolly a time would they have had, that by dinner-time they must have been seriously inebriated. I wonder if the females had as much fun – I doubt it, gossip and tea, not quite the same; and then having to endure the men's high spirits throughout dinner!

According to Booth, the Colonel enjoyed everyone's esteem; he was the same bluff, good-natured friend to all. He knew nothing of class-distinction, that most Victorian conceit. Convivial in his habits, he had a rough wit and was always to be found in the centre of any merriment going. One anecdote has the Colonel directing his coachman to pull up in front of flower-barrows, which were a common sight around London at this time, to allow the horses to nibble at the greenery, solely because he delighted in listening to the inevitably ensuing strong language of the barrow-boys.[7]

Edmundson in *The Nitrate King,* gives a slightly different version of this event, fictional or otherwise. His account is taken from '*Stories of Colonel North'* in The Leeds Mercury of May16 1896 and in this version the Colonels carriage is blocked in traffic beside a costermonger's cart laden with vegetables. On his coachman's attempt to get their horse out of harm's way, the Colonel declares '*Let him graze*'; '*I want to hear the man swear*'. At the ensuing stream of expletives, the Colonel shouts '*Bravo*', tossing the man a coin that would have bought his whole cart-load, adding '*I thought I was pretty well educated in your line myself, but hang me if you haven't taught me four new adjectives!*'

---

7   Guy Deghy 'Paradise in the Strand' 1958

The Colonel was very much what we would call today, a *party animal*, he was burning the candle at both ends, with his business activities by day and intense *socialising* by night, often into the small hours. At the same time, he was juggling several new business ventures worldwide and simultaneously dealing with his many on-going court cases. To add to his woes, elements of the press, like The Economist, felt it was their duty to scrutinise the Colonel's every business endeavour, in its self-assigned role of *protector* of *the small investor*, against what it saw as the Colonel's more questionable business practices.

# Chapter Six

## 'From the Deserts of Tarapacá to the Grassy Slopes of Avery Hill'[8]

In February 1883, a year after his return from Chile, North took out a 10-year lease, at £550 per annum, from the widowed Mrs. Boyd, who was now living in Eastbourne. He needed a house that would be within easy reach of his office in the city and large enough to both, accommodate his family and entertain in the lavish manner he intended; in every respect Avery Hill was an ideal candidate. As has already been established, there had been a house of some importance on that Avery Hill site for at least a century before Norths arrival. Samuel Bagshaw in his 1848 '*History, Gazetteer and Directory of Kent*', described it as '*a pleasant mansion overlooking an extensive district to the south, one mile from Eltham*'. An inventory drawn up by Mrs Boyd for North in 1884 describes an entrance hall leading to an inner hall giving access to a drawing room, dining room, morning room, school room, library and conservatory. On the first floor: five principal bedrooms, bathroom with copper bath and japanned (metal lacquerwork) shower-bath. In addition, six servants bedrooms, butler's pantry, kitchen etc. Numerous outbuildings, one of which in 1859 had served as a brewery. This was a substantial household.

---

8    Dartford Express article 'Celebrity at Home' 1888

The room which had been the drawing room of the original house and was subsequently used as North's library (off the Sculpture Gallery) is, supposedly, the only original room remaining from the original 1841 house and when later drawing up plans for the reconstruction, North insisted this room be incorporated within the new structure and happily it survives to this day.

North's third child Arthur Jewell North had been born in September of 1883, providing a further incentive for the acquisition of a larger house and North, having attained great wealth during his time in Chile, also needed a house commensurate with his aspirations for acceptance into *society*. This was not entirely without ulterior motives, as any social connections would also prove useful in his business dealings. And we thought we had invented *networking!*

In March 1885, North, received the honorary title of *Colonel*, having funded the establishment of the 2nd Tower Hamlets Engineer Volunteer Corps. North was extremely proud of his *title*, so much so, that he was known by that prefix for the rest of his life. One can imagine the scoffing amongst the Colonel's many detractors in the financial press, for whom this must have seemed a forerunner of the '*cash for honours*' of recent times. However, nothing could diminish the Colonel's pride in donning the full military regalia of his new *title* and the popular Spectator cartoon by Spy, shows him sporting epaulettes, cockaded hat and ceremonial sword, chin up, chest out, feet apart – for all the world the model of Gilbert and Sullivans '*Modern Major General*'. A popular subject for many caricaturists of the day, including Harry Furniss, Max Beerbohm and especially Phil May, the Colonel was also a rich source of material for writers of the popular Music Hall songs of the period, many of them parodies of Gilbert and Sullivan, who were at the height of their popularity at the time. One such parody supposedly imagined the scene at Mersey Docks on the departure of Colonel North on his final trip to Chile in 1889:-

*With apologies to Messrs Gilbert & Sullivan!*
*Oh smile not at our grief intense*
*We all adore your affluence*
*And hoped to thrive at your expense*
*But now you leave our English shore*
*Which makes us 'nobs' and nobles roar*
*Oh come back soon we all implore*
*Then we may get thy tips once more*
*Oh Colonel North why do you go away so*
*We only care thy wealth to share*
*Although we may not say so*

The Colonel proved a lavish host for his men of the *Volunteer Corps*, with the extensive grounds at Avery Hill providing ample accommodation for many weekend summer camps, where the Colonel would happily mingle with up to 300 men and officers from the Tower Hamlets regiment. These would have arrived by train at Eltham Station (now Mottingham), where they were met by their Colonel (no doubt in full ceremonial dress). Provisions for such a large body of guests would have been supplied by the farm which formed part of the Avery Hill property. The house and grounds on these occasions were illuminated by many thousands of oil lamps and must have presented a wonderful spectacle for those men of the Corps whose normal surroundings would have been the drab, grey, tree-less streets of London's East End. During the day there would be sports of all kinds with generous £50 prizes for the winners (according to '*The King of Avery Hill*'). The evenings culminated in fireworks and music provided by the regimental band. The Colonel bore the full expense of these annual camps which continued for many years and which, both he and his guests seemed to enjoy immensely. However, these didn't always end happily as there are many newspaper accounts in Oct 1890 of the Colonel having suffered a '*serious accident*' following one of these occasions. Apparently, he was returning from having seen off the Volunteers at Eltham station, when his stirrup leather broke and he was thrown from his horse. He was conveyed home by carriage, where he was attended by his physician Dr. Jeken, who found him to have sustained two broken bones in his fore-arm.

North really did make the most of his rural retreat at Avery Hill even before the renovations, delighting in showing visitors around his pig and poultry farms and on a more fragrant note, the prize roses and camellias lovingly tended by beloved daughter Emma.

Image 7; Emma on the Terrace Avery Hill

While the newspapers of the time were full of spurious tales of the Colonel and his wealth, we can recognise pure fantasy when they cite a story, as The Irish Society of 16<sup>th</sup> Aug 1890 did, claiming that the Colonel had a pond sunk in the grounds of his house (they say in Henley but that is where he had a houseboat) and filled with champagne for the children to ply row boats in! I am quite sure the Colonel would never have wasted good liquor in such a manner.

In addition to the native palms and cacti, the Colonel had also brought back an alpaca goat, a llama and a vicuna, which look like a small camel/llama cross, all natives of South America, and these along with Jacko the tame monkey and his companion the badger, were to be found wandering amongst the native flocks of sheep and cattle at Avery Hill. There is a very endearing, informal portrait of the Colonel in an 1888 article reprinted in The Express (a local Dartford paper), which had originally appeared in *The World – Celebrity at Home*. It paints a charming portrait of the Colonel relaxing at home, of course this is the old Avery Hill house prior to any alteration/extension, and it is described here as '*a long low house covered in wisteria*'. The Colonel, sporting the red-and-blue blazer of the Tower Hamlets Reserves, topped by a broad straw sombrero,' *is sitting on his shady verandah, chatting with friends, including John Whiteley (Director General of the Italian Exhibition) and business partner Robert Harvey. Nothing can be pleasanter than the prospect of Sidcup Woods and the spires of Chislehurst in the distance'*. The author paints a lovely picture of the Colonel surround by his dogs:-

> '*Victor the burly St Bernard (whose transports the Colonel calms with characteristic vigour), Venus the sedate mastiff, Dot the tiny toy-terrier, Bizzy the spaniel and Saub the Chinese 'puzzle' all assisting uninvited at the Cabinet Council of the Nitrates.'*

These wandering animals sometimes ventured further afield and there is an amusing account in the Yorkshire Post of 26<sup>th</sup> Jan 1889 recounting just such an event:-

*'CURIOUS ACTION AGAINST COLONEL At Woolwich. An application has been made to Mr Marsham for summons against Colonel North, of Avery Hill, Eltham for having, November, allowed 30 cattle to stray the highway, and, consequence thereof, impounded in a greenyard in Eltham, kept by Charles Brookes, whereby be became indebted to the said Charles Brooker in the sum of £1.10s., for his reasonable fees and charges. It was stated that a police sergeant, new to the neighbourhood, and unacquainted with Colonel Norths herd cattle, found them unattended on the high road, and drove them to the greenyard, where they were claimed next day by Colonel North's bailiff. The keeper of the greenyard claimed his fee, but did not feel justified in detaining the cattle of an owner so well known as Colonel North, and released them in expectation that the fee would subsequently be paid. It appeared, however, that Colonel North was of the belief that his cattle, which are a peculiar kind, were known throughout the district, and the police, and considering that they might have been as well driven home rather than to the greenyard, refused to pay the fees, and intimated that he was prepared to defend this action. Mr. Marsham expressed doubt whether the poundkeeper could demand his fee after letting the cattle go. The law authorised him to keep stray animals until they paid for, and having parted with the security be must take the consequence-. The Solicitor, however, pressed his application for summons, and said he would undertake the responsibility establishing his case, whereupon Mr. Marsham granted the summons, remarking that the complainant must be prepared to pay costs if he failed.'*

This is a typical example of the contrariness of the Colonel, who was generous to a fault when it was not solicited, but dug his heels in when he thought he was being crossed – he was always quick to litigate but on this one he was bound to lose and all for the sake of £1 10s. This episode also shows his arrogance in expecting his cattle could roam free on the assumption that even his cattle, like himself, would be instantly recognisable!

While enjoying living at Avery Hill, with ample room to house his greyhounds and stabling for his racehorses, the house was just not *grand* enough for a man of substance like the Colonel, intent on making his mark on society. He already had a vast circle of business friends and acquaintances and while he was quite happy to organise lavish entertainments at the Hotel Metropole by Trafalgar Square, he hankered after a house in which he could entertain in real style, one that was worthy of his position as one of the richest men in the world.

In 1888, events conspired to hasten North's plans to create his dream house. An Italian Exhibition was held at Earls Court, of which North was President of the Reception Committee. North probably came by this appointment as a Leeds school-friend of his John Whitley (whose father Joseph ran an engineering firm in Hunslet), was Director General of this same event. By the end of the 19th century London was in the grip of *exhibition fever*. Ambitious events aimed at large-scale audiences curious to find out more about *exotic* cultures, were held in the capital in vast public arenas such as Earls Court and Olympia in West London and the Crystal Palace in South London. The Italian Exhibition would prove pivotal in North's quest for his 'ideal home'. Although not professing to be a connoisseur of the arts, North took the opportunity to buy several works including both paintings and sculptures. The exhibition seems to have made a marked impression, as having met the architect Thomas William Cutler there, he left determined to build himself a mini-palace in the *Italianate* style at Avery Hill. He had the money to realise his dream and Cutler would now give form to the Colonel's aspirations. Before leaving on his triumphal final visit to Chile in 1889, North engaged Cutler to carry out *'additions and alterations'* to the house at Avery Hill, up to a figure of £30,000, which soon became £40,000 – all these being *verbal* agreements. The main building contractor engaged for the works was a Mr. J. Chappell of Pimlico.

On North's return to England, Cutler was quick to inform him that costs had escalated to £65,000 during his absence, but assured the Colonel that this figure would not be exceeded. However, North was soon appraised that the bill for his *renovations* would likely amount to £115,000, at which point Cutler was dismissed and his assistant J. O. Cook took over. Cook was a local man, having been born in Plumstead in 1852, and it would have been convenient for the Colonel to have Cutler's successor at close proximity for the duration of the work and also for maintenance of the new-fangled electrics once the house was completed. Cook was described as *assistant architect*, but he was in fact a Chartered Surveyor (which accounts for me not being able to locate him in RIBA archives) for a partnership in Woolwich and it must have seemed like a poisoned chalice he had accepted from Cutler. However, from details in a family memoir by C.B. Mears written in 1991 entitled *The Cooks of Bostall*, it seems that Cook was particularly good at estimating costs and subsequently keeping to them, which was exactly what the Colonel was looking for, having sacked Cutler for failing to do just that. The fact that he was not an architect facilitated his taking over from Cutler, as the RIBA Code of Conduct would not allow for one member of to supplant another. Aged 38, Cook was 11 years younger than Cutler at the time when Avery Hill was being re-modelled. Mears suggests in his *Cook Family Memoir,* that Cook was already known to Colonel North prior to his sacking of Cutler as he mentions members of the Cook family attending a Boxing Day 1887 party at Avery Hill. He suggests this was probably due to the fact that Cook's employers H.H. Church & Partners were the only surveyors/architects to be found in local directories and the Colonel would have wanted a local company to oversee any maintenance required on Avery Hill as stipulated in his lease from Mrs. Boyd, prior to his purchasing the property. Mears acknowledges that the re-modelling of Avery Hill would have normally been out of Cook's league. However, Cutler's original drawings and plan seem to have been followed quite precisely and it would have been comforting for the Colonel to have a local man on call in an emergency. It does look like all works on Avery Hill proceeded in a timely fashion and more importantly perhaps, on-budget with Cook as supervising *architect.* Any savings were of course offset by the Colonel's subsequent lawsuit with Cutler.

Cutler sued the Colonel for £2,718 commission outstanding, with the Colonel counter-claiming *'excessive charges'* and delays in completion. One has to agree with the judge on this occasion, who asked why the Colonel had not formally limited expenditure at £30,000 – North countering that *'he thought he was dealing with a gentleman'*. And having paid out all the money that he did, why balk at Cutler's comparatively modest commission? But that is the Colonel all over, careless with large sums and then litigious over small. It is indeed extraordinary that an astute businessman like North could have allowed his building costs to have spiralled out of control so negligently. An eminent architect of the day, Charles Barry Jn., whose father, also Charles had designed the rebuilt Palace of Westminster, or Houses of Parliament as they are commonly known, assisted by Augustus Pugin in the 1830's, was called as an expert witness in the court hearing. Barry estimated that using sketch plans produced by Cutler, he would have estimated the works at nearer to £80,000 – twice what Cutler had said.

The jury concurred and awarded in Cutler's favour. The judge, Lord Coleridge, concluded that North was *'an overbearing person, accustomed to have his own way'*. Some felt that Coleridge was overly harsh with the Colonel, but the judge probably rightly thought our Colonel had had too much to say for himself having slandered both Cutler and the architect profession in general, and had suggested that *'he must behave himself in court as though he were the poorest subject of the Queen'*. He also observed (tongue in cheek) that the Colonel was not such a man as to concern himself with budgets, the things that *'poor human creatures with only £30,000 or £40,000 a year were obliged to'*. *'Build me a house!'* he decreed, it was then the responsibility of others to realise his vision. Judge Coleridge's criticism of the Colonel's *'ungentlemanly'* remarks about his former architect in no way deflated the conceit or dimmed the unbridled self-confidence of *The Nitrate King*.

It is worth saying here that Cutler seems to have not always been so profligate with his client's money, as in 1896 the Hotel Metropole Folkestone, for which he was the architect, was opened, having cost a modest £150,000, despite being lavishly appointed and accommodating 250 guests.[9] Maybe he was a good architect and not such a good project manager. Franklin in 'Country Houses', observes that for many reasons, the final bill for building works would be far more than the estimate - even so, the costs incurred in the building works at Avery Hill still seem steep when compared to those of other *gentlemen's country houses* featured in Franklin's book. She tells us that a country house could be built at this time at the lower end for between £7,000-£10,000 with Waterhouse's remodelling of Eaton Hall for the Duke of Westminster coming in at the top end at £600,000. Most seem to have been in the £50,000-£100,000 bracket, including Nathan's brother-in-law, Ferdinand de Rothschild's Waddesdon Manor where the Prince of Wales was indeed a frequent guest, with his mother Queen Victoria bestowing a visit in 1890. Waddesdon was described by Phyllida Barstow in *The English Country House Party* as '*halfway between French chateau and oriental palace*'. Nathan's brother Alfred's Halton House near Wendover was altogether another matter, being described by Virginia Coules in her history of the Rothschild Family '*The Rothschilds: A Family of Fortune*'[10] as '*An exaggerated nightmare* of gorgeousness and senseless and ill-applied magnificence'. At a time of pervasive anti-semitism amongst the upper-classes, rumour had it that the POW relied on his Jewish banker friends like the Rothschild's and Sir Ernest Cassel for financial advice, some went as far as claiming that they even settled his many debts. This mutually beneficial arrangement meant the POW enjoyed lavish hospitality while he ensured their acceptance in society. Queen Victoria kept a tight rein on the POW as she was aware of his profligate nature and consequently, most of those in the POW's circle had much more disposable income than the heir to the throne himself.

Booth in '*Palmy Days*' remarked of the Colonel:-

> '*A strange mixture of business and financial capacity, and in his personal affairs, sheer carelessness in money matters, the Colonel inevitably was on occasion a loser*'

9    The Builder Dec 18th 1909 pg 678
10   Virginia Coules 'The Rothschilds: A Family of Fortune' Hamish Hamilton 1973

And nowhere was this more evident than in the Colonel's lack of oversight concerning expenditure on the refurbishment of Avery Hill.

# Chapter Seven

## Final Trip to Chile 1889; Balmaceda

Given all the various projects and accompanying law-suits, I think it is fair to assume that by this time the Colonel must have been under severe strain, even for one of his obvious physical as well as psychological strength. However, this trip had to be undertaken in order to show his commitment to the nitrate industry and calm the market, and he was probably keen to re-visit the country which had proved so pivotal in his fortunes.

The trip to Chile in Feb 1889 was essentially to calm the nerves of British nitrate investors, as rumours had been circulating, that there was no underlying substance to the Colonels commercial enterprises and that these were no more than a sham. There was also the pressing need to establish exactly what President Balmaceda's intentions were in regard to the nitrate industry, in addition Balmaceda had been making threats to break North's monopoly with his Nitrate Railways Company. In order to have an independent account of this journey and its findings, he took along with him two journalists, William Howard Russell from The Times, the other from The Financial Times and an artist, Melton Prior from the Illustrated London News, to record their findings, independent of any interference from North himself. Russell was a seasoned war correspondent having covered the Crimean War for The Times in 1854-5 and Melton Prior was a war artist having covered the Boer War for The Illustrated London News. The account was subsequently published in 1890 as '*A Visit to* Chile *and the Nitrate Fields of Tarapacá*' by William Howard Russell with Melton Prior's illustrations.

Russell said that he was tempted by this trip, as despite his many travels he had never been further south than Panama. North was to be accompanied on the trip by his daughter Emma and they were to be joined in New York by Mrs. North, Harry and the Colonel's brother Gamble for the return journey to England. 20 year-old Emma, was accompanied on this trip by her friend Miss Wentworth-Smith and it shows a truly adventurous spirit that two cosseted Victorian females should be embarking on a journey that would take them across the ocean to a desert landscape prone to earthquake, through bandit territory and up alligator-infested rivers. I can just see her mother Jane, reaching for the smelling-salts when told that her daughter Emma was to accompany her father on this trip!

The North party which numbered about ten people in total, sailed from Liverpool on the *SS Galicia* and before embarking, North delivered a speech to assembled journalists and well-wishers outside the Adelphi Hotel in which he described his nemesis, The Financial News, as a '*blackmailing*' paper and judging by this article, he was probably justified. The Financial News was one of North's consistent critics. Founded in 1884 by Harry Marks, the paper described itself as "*a trusted guide of the investing public*" and set out to expose fraudulent investments. John Thomas North became a favourite target. The mutual enmity reached boiling point early in 1889, just as North was preparing to undertake his return trip to Chile, and was described in the paper thus:-

'*He was heard lamenting there were not more elements in nature than air, earth and water, as they were such nice things to finance.*

*In Tarapacá he has made himself master of all the existing elements. With his Nitrate Companies and Nitrate Railways he controls all the saleable earth in the province. With his sea-water condensers, his water barrels and his Pica concession he monopolises the drinking materials. It is generally understood that [recently] he was elaborating a scheme for placing the atmosphere of Tarapacá under the care of a limited liability company, with an airy capital of several millions sterling.'*

The Financial News, June 14, 1888

By the time Harry Marks heard the *'blackmailing'* calumny, North and his party had already sailed (or steamed). Cartoonists then had a field day, when Mr. Marks, supposedly offered a reward of £1000 to any boat that might overtake Norths, in order to deliver a writ for slander. This was not technically possible, as North's vessel was steam-powered and therefore much faster than any of the Liverpool *tugs* in the port and what is more, North's ship had several hours start.

It was hoped that this trip would also serve to clarify North's own misgivings concerning the political situation, with Chilean President Balmaceda making disparaging speeches about *'foreigners'* controlling his country's nitrate industry and mutterings of an imminent nationalisation of the industry and the railways serving it. By 1890 British nitrate investors led by North, controlled 60% of nitrate output, which had brought them to Balmaceda's attention, however he was pragmatic enough to acknowledge that a reduction in output would negatively affect both tax revenues and worker's wages, while boosting the research for a synthetic substitute for nitrate. North came bearing gifts of two through-bred horses from Mr. Burdett-Coutts stud, a complete fire-engine for the city of Iquique, and a commemorative shield bearing the inscription *'To the Republic of Chile. John T. North'*, which he intended to present to President Balmaceda. The shield held a relic of the ship *'Esmeralda'* and bore a star on its capstan - a national symbol for the Chilean people. During the War of the Pacific. The

Chilean ship *Esmeralda* had engaged with the much larger Peruvian vessel the *Huascar*, during the naval battle of Iquique and was sunk with its captain dying heroically with his ship. North had specifically engaged the services of an experienced diver in order to retrieve items from the sunken *Esmeralda;* had he just wanted to make a lavish but empty gesture, I feel he would not have gone to such lengths to present something with such significance to the Chilean consciousness. The Colonel also had a copy of this shield made which he kept himself at Avery Hill as a memento.

Many accounts at the time claimed that North's gifts were snubbed by both Chile and its President, however William Russell claims not to have seen such evidence. North hoped that Russell as an independent journalist would see for himself the substance of his nitrate enterprises and the transformation they had made in creating a thriving industrial complex in the heart of the desert of Tarapaća and would be able to convince the many sceptics (topping the list The Financial News and The Economist), who were convinced that North's empire was mainly *smoke and mirrors* accompanied by a large dose of North *bluster*. There were those who questioned the impartiality of Russell's reports, but it is unlikely that he would have jeopardised his own reputation in order to save North's, moreover, he had only undertaken the assignment with the assurance that he would be a totally independent observer.

Russell and his wife joined the *Galicia* at Lisbon. He tells us that the North party had many ways of passing the time during the long voyage. There was a daily lottery to guess how many miles had been covered in any one day, with the average being 300. The Colonel organised games on deck including tennis, cricket and running races and the vessel's lowlier passengers of *'foreigners and several hundred emigrants'* were much bemused at the running and jumping of these supposedly reserved English men and women above decks – those below decks numbered about 400-500 mainly Italian immigrants bound for Argentina. A young Irishman named Manders, who was headed for Patagonia to breed horses, proved to be the champion runner on board

- we can just imagine the Colonel, red in the face, as he attempts to outstrip his younger, fitter opponent. We also hear of a M. Bottoni, with his multiple accomplishments – poet, cornet-player and skillful dancer. During the day, the men would amuse themselves by shooting at anything unwise enough to show itself above water and the day's entertainment would invariably end with song and dance till lights out.

Image 8; North party on deck of Galicia - Colonel(seated left), Emma (centre holding book)

Divine service was conducted every Sunday with one passenger observing that he did not find the English any better for all their Sunday praying and singing - they came out to make money and in his opinion, they drank and swore, gambled, quarreled and cheated just like other people. Russell does not mention the incident which one newspaper subsequently published of Miss Emma being admonished by the Captain for whistling on the Sabbath, so we must treat that story with a degree of scepticism, even though it is quite amusing, as are all of the dubious North myths.

On 27th Feb 1889, the *Galicia* anchored in Rio de Janeiro, stopping for supplies and re-fueling, having spent 21 days at sea. Russell recalls seeing a book-shop window there displaying placards illustrating the terrible deeds of *Jack the Ripper* and how this served to curtail any feeling of English superiority he may have been feeling wandering amongst the squalor of low-life Rio. The party headed for the relative clean air of higher ground and Whytes Hotel, where a good supper and clean beds awaited. We are given a description of the beautiful surroundings - tall palms sheltering flowers with their blaze of colour and the attendant brightly-hued butterflies *'some as* large *as thrushes'*. Humming-birds hanging like bright petals from leaves and flashing jewel-like from shrub to shrub. A stream running through the hotel grounds allowed for a swim before breakfast, with strict segregation of the ladies and gentlemen.

Image 9; Whyte's Hotel Tijuca

Returning to ship, they now proceeded to Montevideo in Uruguay where the port authorities would not allow any passengers to disembark, due to fears of yellow fever as the ship had touched down in Rio, where this scourge was raging, so passengers could be unwitting carriers. To compensate for this disappointment, the *jolly* Colonel, who could always be relied on to come up with some diversion, organised a ball on board ship - having the deck festooned with flags of all nations, it was swiftly transformed into a '*dancing saloon*' – we can imagine Emma North and her chaperone friend were very much in demand as dance partners. Colonel North was indeed a great *events organiser,* even at sea*!*

We learn that the *Galicia* provided excellent board and lodging, with fresh milk, butter, bread, meat, vegetables and poultry and even ice to cool passenger's drinks, those above decks anyway. Landing in Coronel in Chile on 16th March, they were welcomed by a great crowd of North's friends, who had travelled far just to welcome their friend the Colonel and his party. While walking around the town, Russell is surprised at its prosperity, with shopfronts displaying German, Italian, Spanish and English names. The inhabitants seemed comfortable and well-ordered and their situation is compared favourably to '*squalid towns on the coast of an island nearer England*' – Is he referring to Ireland?

The party are given a ride on a special train of the Arauco Railway (North owned,) which gave Russell his first chance of assessing North's investments at close quarters and he certainly seems to have been positively impressed. He recalls Colonel North mentioning that he and a Mr. Abbott, whose company was contracted to build the Arauco Railway, were '*fellow workmen on the coast at $1 a day six-and-twenty years ago*' – which would be 1863, six years before North's arrival in Peru - so it must be wistful exaggeration. All the machinery for the construction of the Arauco Railway came, whenever possible from Leeds, another example of North always seeking to support his native town.

Their journey now continued on a Chilean ship *Chiloe* to Valparaiso, where North has his first meeting with President Balmaceda. Foreign investors had been alarmed by a new policy of the President's - *'Chile for the Chileans,'* which was the title of the speech he delivered on his recent tour round the country. However, Balmaceda, allayed these fears by declaring at the meeting, that he welcomed foreign capital in the development of the country's resources and that he had no intention of waging war on vested interests. He went on to praise the Nitrate Railway, which he had visited at Iquique, much to the satisfaction of Colonel North. Nevertheless, members of the Chilean press who were present, seem to have been of the opinion that these assurances were not in the gift of the President and any future railway extension was under the auspices of the Government and any decision would be reserved for the State. Balmaceda was subsequently portrayed as having overstepped his powers, thereby impinging on the constitutional rights of his government.

The North party now continued by train to Santiago where again, many well-wishers had assembled to welcome the Colonel. North needed to attend to some business prior to proceeding on to the nitrate works at Tarapacá, he would be well aware of any price movements in nitrate on the stock markets during his absence, as each day the ship made telegraph contact with London and Liverpool to establish stock and share prices. The party checked in to the Hotel Oddo, which was soon besieged with *'ladies of mournful aspect, their heads wrapped in mantas, some with babes in their arms, all with petitions and supplications for the boundlessly wealthy, generous English Colonel'*[11]

Another meeting with President Balmaceda followed, to which North was accompanied by his friend and business associate Mr. Dawson, and a Mr. Manby. The President raised the issue of North's recent purchase of the *Las Lagunas* nitrate field at well below market value, from a Chilean gentleman whose right to sell was questionable. Despite this, the President professed to be anxious for foreign capitalists to push forward the railway expansion. It seems Balmaceda was stuck between a rock and a hard place, wanting to be pragmatic but also wishing to appear to

---

11   William Howard Russell 'A Trip to Chile......' pg 89

be doing right by his countrymen. Afterwards, Russell describes a drive to the suburbs of Santiago:-

> 'a cry of dogs, mongrels of low degree; men lounging about the grogshops; broken windows; ragged poultry skirmishing in the highway; kennel-like huts of reeds, lath-and-plaster, patched with bits of corrugated iron and zinc…women with black matted locks, ill-favoured and ill-dressed, with a fierce look in the eye and a defiant air'[12]

Russell, who seems to have had an *eye for the ladies,* is not much impressed by the charms of the ladies of Santiago.

A mild earthquake was experienced during their time in Santiago but the unflappable Mrs. Russell, who must have been used to foreign travel with her husband being a war correspondent, was unfazed, although the room trembled, utensils clinked and there was a sensation *like the rumbling of an underground train.* At breakfast that morning, only one other member of their party had noticed the phenomenon, while their host pronounced it '*only a temblor'.*

Russell remarks again on the preponderance of English names like Morgan, Jones, Wilson and Barry. He mentions travelling in the tracks of Charles Darwin from Santiago to Cauqueness, a journey that took them three-and-a-half hours by train, and Darwin two days, on horseback or carriage. There was an abundance of very palatable Chilean wine and pilsener beer – at this time the European market for wine would have been dominated by the French, whereas now New World (including Chile) has probably overtaken in popularity.

Emma North seems to have accompanied her father on at least some of his field inspections, as Melton Prior's illustration below of Emma with her father during a plant inspection attests. A week was spent at a mineral baths, a *Chilean Carlsbad,* as Russell describes it, where there

---

12   Ibid   pg 92

Image 10; Leaving Cauquenes Gen. Baquedano with Colonel North & Emma

were separate marble baths for men and women, fed by the mineral springs of Cauquenes, which were reputedly effective in the treatment of rheumatism, eczema and throat infections – this sounds very much like the Colonel's own Turkish Bath which Cutler was busily (and expensively) constructing in his absence. Music and dancing followed at night, but no gambling or cards, Russell adds rather ruefully. Gambling was one of the main attractions at the European spas, hence their popularity with the ruling classes, especially our own Prince of Wales, whose mother Queen Victoria kept a tight rein on his allowance, being well aware of her son's failings.

A *fête champêtre*, or garden party was organised at which '*the natives and strangers fraternised most warmly, and song and dance wound up the pleasures of the day – indeed the people we met in our travels always seemed ready to join in any junketing in their way*'.[13] Exactly the sort of boon-

---

13    Ibid   pg 107

companions the Colonel would be delighted to find himself amongst. The next jaunt was a visit to a cattle-ranch owned by a Sénor Soto, where they were regaled with a thrilling display of the skills of the *vaqueras* (cowboys), most of the gentlemen in the audience being horsemen, were well impressed with the dexterity with which these South American cowboys rounded and corralled the animals. There were 190 *vaqueras* and 500 workers families living on S. Soto's estate, along with many thousands of cattle, sheep and horses. Russell is so impressed that he suggests '*There cannot be a finer raw material for cavalry than the Chilean peasantry, in the world'*.[14] North, master of the Master of the Mid-Kent Stag Hunt, would have been in his element.

The party now proceeded to Valparaiso, where again, the Colonel was besieged by calls on his charity, again mostly women in straitened circumstances. They had been encouraged by the many biographies and portraits of the Nitrate King that had been published in every town following North's progress on his nitrate tour, with reports of his enormous wealth. Apparently, it was in the nature of Chileans to be charitable amongst themselves and therefore they found it quite reasonable to appeal to a rich man who had made his fortune in Chile.

On May 1st the North party proceeded towards Iquique and the *Nitrate Kingdom* by steamer. Arriving at Huasco, they made for Carrizal, which was one of the places that Colonel North was first employed having arrived in Peru in search of his fortune. He led his friends to a deserted workshop, '*There is the bench at which I worked! There is the place where I kept my tools! Here, day after day for many a month, I worked as an engineer at four dollars a day!*'[15] We can easily picture the enterprising young J.T. North with his imagination working overtime as he formulated money-making prospects while he toiled away at his workbench. Russell recounts that the visit to Carrizal was a high-point in the trip for the Colonel, prompting memories of his early days on that Continent.

---

14   Ibid   pg 109
15   William Howard Russell 'A trip to Chile....'   Pg 135

The party's arrival in Iquique, main port for the nitrate trade, on 7th May, drew a large crowd of both Chilean and English friends, intent on honouring the man who had done so much for their town. The visit began with an inspection of the Tarapaća Foundry which seems to have been owned by the firm of North, Humphrey & Dickinson (North's sister Emma's son-in-law?). Here, three to four hundred men were engaged in making the machinery necessary to the running of the nitrate works and the Nitrate Railway. Colonel North presents the town of Iquique with the prize Exhibition fire-engine, which they had brought with them from England, as a present to the town. This town, like all the others in the region, being built of wood, had suffered severely from fires hence the preponderance of fire-brigades. In addition to the storage of many highly flammable materials, nitrate of soda had a particular propensity to spontaneously combust, a phenomena which they had yet to find an explanation for. Many nitrate-laden ships had caught fire, much to the consternation of Lloyds Insurers, who must therefore have been levying heavy premiums for their cover. Russell mentions the superior administration under Chilean rule and was told '*Chilean officials are honest and Peruvian officials the reverse*'. In his opinion the Chileans were earnest in their endeavours to improve conditions in their country. From their quarters in a Mr. Rowland's house (we are not told exactly who this man is, he must be associated with the railway), there was a good view of the comings and goings on the Nitrate Railway, enabling Russell to satisfy the naysayers back home, some of whom disputed it's very existence!. We are informed that Fairlie & Fowler (young North's Leeds employer) engines pulled the nitrate-laden cars with great ease; powerful engines were essential as the terrain had very steep gradients. Fowlers produced all the rolling-stock and engines for the Nitrate Railway, and again evidence of North's determination that he should use his position to benefit his native county Leeds at every opportunity, by patronising the company of his old employer.

North then took the party to inspect the *Buen Retiro* plant, with Russell remarking that from the outside, it looked remarkably similar to a north-country coal mine, with its tall chimneys and corrugated iron

buildings, and a high bank of refuse. What with the *caliche* (raw nitrate-bearing rock) crushers and condensers working night and day, and the flames from the boilers piercing the night sky, it must have seemed like a veritable home-from-home for the *'humble mechanic from Leeds'*, and further evidence to Russell of the very real and extensive substance of North's nitrate enterprises.

Once nitrate-bearing deposits were identified in the field, the beds were then blown with explosives (See Image 5), to allow access for the men who then used large iron bars to separate the nitrate-bearing rock from the rest and loaded this into wagons for transporting to the plant for processing.

There were further inspectional trips to two more North properties, the *Ramirez* (now transferred to the Liverpool Nitrate Company) and the *Primitiva* plants, where more tumultuous receptions awaited. The

Ramirez had at one time been the largest nitrate producing establishment in Chile. The manager of the *Primitiva*, a Mr. Humberstone accommodated the party in his own house, which Russell likened to '*a good Indian bungalow*' – it must have been commodious to have held the North party, but Russell voices a suspicion that some of its permanent inhabitants may have had to double-up in order to accommodate their esteemed guests. With the nitrate works being less than a hundred yards distance and the house being on an elevated position, there was a good view of the workings and of the large village of one-storeyed houses where the workmen and their families lived. In the comfort of Mr. Humberstone's abode, Russell says it was hard to imagine one was '*in a house on a waterless desert, or to understand how, in a few years, so many of the conveniences and luxuries of life, could have been collected on the spot*'.[16] What had been a lifeless waste at the opening of the nineteenth century was now '*a centre of enterprise, capital, science and civilisation*'.[17]

The plant worked round the clock with shifts of workers. *Primitiva* was vast, covering twelve square miles.

---

16   William Howard Russell 'A trip to Chile....' Pg 177
17   Ibid. Pg 192

Image 12; Primitiva plant

Russell observes *'It is touching to see how the traditions of the English household assert themselves under adverse circumstances. There is in every English house, the drawing-room with mirrors, sofa, tables covered with albums, the piano, flowers in vases....'* The difference being that the children of the house may have a *'sleek llama with a soft black curling coat'* rather than the dog which their counterparts back home had to make do with. The Norths had both of course, roaming the grounds back home at Avery Hill.

One may imagine that the ladies in the party might have been bored during their stay at the nitrate plant but there were plenty of diversions, with balls organised between the neighbouring nitrate plants at Iquique and Pisagua, with legions of cooks and musicians brought in by train – very reminiscent of one of the Colonel's famous *entertainments* at Avery Hill. During the day there were carriage rides, picnics and excursions where they were able to fraternise with the resident ladies of the nitrate community, who were probably intrigued to hear talk of *'back home'* – Emma and her companion were probably even more eager to hear what life was like for these ladies stranded as they were in the middle of the desert!.

One day ended with an improvised ball at the house of a neighbour, with some of the English guests attempting the native dance, the *samacuecca*, which the British community dubbed the *Quaker*. This is amusing, as Russell goes on to describe the dance, with castanets and handkerchief, as being very much like *flamenco*, and having an underlying intent *'decidedly carnal'* – followers of the Quaker religion were notoriously pious and puritanical.

As has already been said, Russell's primary mission was to allay investor fears by independent attestation to the existence and viability of the nitrate investments. He apologises to the reader who may not be so interested in the minutiae of nitrate production but he could not have rendered a true account of his travels through the *Nitrate Kingdom* without mention of the underlying processes as he was there to attest to the profitability of the industry along with other members of the group. He compares the relative un-profitability of the Chilean-run nitrate plants created by the government in an attempt to take back control of nitrate production – much like nationalised industries in the UK have always been huge loss-makers.

On one excursion, Russell remarks having seen hieroglyphics on a hill, '*Inca marks*' he was told, and wonders how there could have been interest for anyone to venture into '*this outspread crust of salt*'. He mentions the discomfort of being covered in salt particles when proceeding across the nitrate fields on horseback.

In the event, it was found that Balmaceda's chest-thumping was more for his domestic audience, and when confronted with hostility in the British press and the disapproval of the British government, he adopted a more conciliatory tone knowing that his nitrate revenues depended on foreign investment and technical know-how. He must also have been well aware that Britain took 67% of Chile's exports while accounting for 43% of her imports. In John Mayo's 1981 '*Britain and Chile 1851-1886: Anatomy of a Relationship*' he claims that what the British did was to link Chile with the world economy from which the Republic gained financially as well as in the modernisation of that economy. Mayo apportions blame instead to the Chilean elites who preferred to invest in mining and banking rather than nitrates.

The President's assurance of not wanting to upset the status-quo were understandably music to the Colonel's ears. Balmaceda seemed to have lost favour amongst the Chilean working classes when he failed to deliver the salary increases he had promised – seeming more popular with the Chilean ruling class. Contrary to many leftist historical accounts, the workers had willingly joined forces with insurgents to topple Balmaceda, without any encouragement from British nitrate interests. In 1890, Balmaceda sent soldiers to suppress a strike in the nitrate region and then in 1891, Balmaceda supporting soldiers clashed with workers at

North's Ramirez plant, leaving fifteen workers dead, giving fuel to the idea that Balmaceda – loyal forces had been instrumental in a massacre of nitrate workers.

Meanwhile back home, The Dartford Express of 28<sup>th</sup> Dec 1889 would claim that North's recent trip to South America had cost £20,000 and was a '*sort of Argonautic expedition*' - referring to Jason and the Argonauts (of Greek Mythology) quest for the Golden Fleece. They go on to report a curious incident during the voyage, when Emma was reprimanded by one of the quartermasters for apparently whistling a tune on *the Sabbath*. North was supposedly most upset that his daughter should be subjected to what he considered to be an indignity and complained to the captain who, as one would expect, supported his subordinate saying that he was only upholding the rules of the ship regarding respectful observation of the Sabbath. Victorian young ladies whistling on *the Sabbath* – what was the world coming to?!!

Much as I would like to believe this story, I have to discount it as I feel sure Russell would have mentioned it in his account '*A Trip to Chile*', unless he was deferring to the Colonel and sparing his daughters blushes.

The party were due to embark on the *Cachapoal* for their return journey on 7<sup>th</sup> June from Iquique and again, the pier was thronged with North well-wishers. On this occasion, those assembled were rewarded with one of the Colonel's heart-rending speeches, where he remembers early friends and their mutual initial hardship prior to attaining success. His words struck a chord in his audience as they were delivered with much emotion, as one would expect from a North speech. As the boat proceeded northwards, Russell remarks seeing several small islands, which as they got closer, turned out to be clumps of many thousands of pelicans. They stopped in Lima, where they were put up at a most comfortable hotel, and a cricket match was organised between the *Cachapoal's* passengers and the British residents of Lima. Russell and his wife, not being cricket-lovers visited Lima Cathedral instead, where the bones of Pizarro, the sixteenth-century Spanish *conquistador,* were interred. Pizarro had conquered the Incas and claimed Peru for the Spanish. Lima was full of reminders of its Spanish colonial past and Russell professes to fin the Peruvian ladies '*possessed of personal attractions which were by no means common in the south.* '[18] This of course is not the first time the 69-year-old Russell has alluded to the charm or otherwise of the ladies encountered on his travels. He declares Lima to be the most interesting place they saw while in South America, not surprising considering the amount of time they had spent visiting nitrate plants in the desert!

During their stay in Lima, the North party were entertained by the British Ambassador, Sir Charles Mansfield and they learnt that they were to be treated to a bull-fight the following day, but unfortunately the captain of the *Cachapoal* received his sailing orders, so they had to forego that pleasure. As their ship proceeded towards Panama, Russell tells us that Miss North '*excited the envy of the anglers on board by capturing a fine Corbino, which could only be got on deck by the use of a big basket as a landing-net*'[19]. Their ship now entered the Guayaquil River, where they proceeded with the help of a pilot. We are told that the Guayaquil had many floating weed-islands, rich with water lilies and flowering shrubs – it was also rich in alligators. They were now passing through Ecuador and the passengers were afforded a final bit of sport as it was decided that they should race another ship the *Pizarro* – I see the Colonel's hand here as we are told he made frequent visits to the boiler-room to offer advice and encouragement as one would expect from an engineer. With the Colonel's sound advice, the *Cachapoal* managed to just edge ahead as Panama came into view. A successful end to what was definitely a successful, and by Russell's account, most enjoyable trip.

The very next day, the North party boarded a steamer for New York where they were joined by Mrs. North, son Harry and JT's brother Gamble North and several other friends from England. Ever the astute

---

18    William Howard Russell 'A Trip to Chile....'   Pg 274
19    William Howard Russell 'A Trip to Chile....'   Pg 276

businessman, North used his time in the United States and Canada, checking out new investment opportunities. The New York Times of July 8th 1889 headline read '*The Nitrate King is Here: A Chilean Monte Cristo on His Travels*'. It was a flattering account, commenting on the Colonel's youthful appearance for his forty-five years, the overall impression of a quiet English gentleman, with the only indication of *nouveaux riches being his 'flashy jewelry'* – it also comments on his strong Yorkshire *burr* despite his many years in a Spanish-speaking country. Apparently he never did learn the Spanish language.

The trip seems to have been successful, at least in the short term, in calming the fears of both domestic investors and President Balmaceda. However, nitrate prices at home, had dropped during the Colonel's absence and the Economist of Aug 3rd 1889, worried of the influence that one man had on the movements in the nitrate markets reports that it was essentially a *one-man market*, with impressionable investors following like sheep, where ever the Colonel might lead them. From the time of his return to England and his death in 1896, North had been connected at one time or another with more than two-thirds of the British nitrate joint-stock companies.

Very much ahead of his time and with great foresight, North had in 1889 created *The Permanent Nitrate Committee* as a public relations vehicle for the promotion of the benefits of nitrate as a fertiliser and to ensure that nitrate remained very much in the public eye by promoting research, placing newspaper adverts and lobbying politicians. However, back in Chile the political landscape became increasingly turbulent and by Jan 1891, President Balmaceda and his Congressional Party were pitted against each other. The ensuing Revolution and war in Chile has been blamed by some South American historians on the Colonel and his Chilean banker associates and this view was supported by *The Times* special correspondent in Chile at the time, Maurice Hervey, who pulled no punches in pointing the finger firmly in North's direction. The fact is that North actually stood to lose from civil war and the inevitable interruption caused to commerce as a result of military action. Leftist Chilean historian, Hernan Ramirez Necochea, in his study of the Chilean Civil War published in 1958, is also unequivocal in apportioning blame on *'a cold calculating capitalist, capable of using all suitable means to fulfil his aims'*. North was also attacked in the Chilean press at the time, who suggested that foreign capital had transformed the nitrate region into a *'kind of English India', 'controlled from outside and leaving the nation with a sovereignty more nominal than real'* El Ferrocarril May 26th 1889.

It is essential to see all of this from an English perspective and what nitrates meant to the British speculative market. After the War of the Pacific, North's energies seem to have been more concentrated on keeping up the price of his nitrate stocks rather than the profits from the underlying assets. North was part of the British world, not the Chilean - he had little reason to launch a civil war against Balmaceda, and the war itself did not preserve his fortune.

Before leaving Chile, North had appointed a lawyer, Julio Zegers, who also happened to be a prominent Liberal politician, to act as a lobbyist and look after his interests in his absence. While North, as one would expect, did everything in his power to protect his business interests in Chile, the modern historical view seems to be that revolution in Chile would have happened even without North's *behind the scenes* machinations. Historian Michael Monteon wrote in 1975 *'that interpretation of the Revolution of 1891 has failed to implicate either the British government or the British merchant sector in London'*. Maurice Zeitlin in his 1984 book *'The Civil Wars in Chile (or the Bourgeois Revolution that Never Was)'* states *'Balmaceda's nationalist policies were undoubtedly crucial in sparking the struggle'* and concludes *'But I reject the narrow thesis that English imperialists (particularly John T.North's nitrate group) and other foreign capitalists generated the opposition and sustained the armed insurrection against Balmaceda'*. It was quite natural that leftist historians would cast Balmaceda as the *martyr* following his suicide in 1891 viewing North as having all the traits of the archetypal *robber baron*. However, this simplification of complex events has not borne recent historical revisionism, which I am generally not a lover of, but in North's case seems justified. A new generation of Chilean historians like Pedro Elizondo and Bernardo Guerrero, see the need for a reappraisal of North's legacy in Chile. They recognise that his engineering skills brought water, machinery and railways to the barren nitrate region, without which Chile would not have been in a position to exploit what turned out to be their main natural resource and benefit from the jobs created and the tax revenues raised. Elizondo went as far as to say *'As a citizen of Iquique, I recognise his merits for what he meant to the province of Tarapaća"*.

Once back in England, North began to diversify into Belgian industry, Australian mines, Congo rubber plantations and Egyptian tramways, while simultaneously divesting himself of some nitrate interests as that market started to show signs of faltering due to over-production and dwindling demand.

# Chapter Eight

## Entertaining-'1 Enjoyed Myself Thoroughly'[20]

The Colonel, as we have already observed, liked nothing better than putting on a *bit of a do*, whether it was for 600 poor children from Westminster, 300 of his Tower Hamlets Volunteers or 1000 of the *great and the good* whether at the Hotel Metropole or at home at Avery Hill once the Mansion was completed. In the Colonel's case, *a bit of a do,* always seemed to turn into *a lot of a do,* as he was not one to stint on hospitality. This penchant for entertaining and general merry-making pre-dates the re-modelling of Avery Hill, with the Colonel organising lavish entertainments at many London hotels, however, the Hotel Metropole seems to have been a particular favourite, with its position in the centre of London and just next to Charing Cross Station.

Mears, in his 1991 family memoir '*The Cooks of Bostall',* mentions members of the Cook family (North's architect Cutler's replacement) attending one of the Colonel's big parties on Boxing Day 1887. Have not been able to locate any other references to this particular party but there definitely was a ball in the Whitehall Rooms of the Metropole on 30th December 1887 and it must be this that the Cook family attended, as to host two balls within the space of days was probably beyond even

---

20   *Sidcup and District Times article 'Death of Colonel North' 8th May 1896*

the Jolly Colonel. A copy of the menu for this event (See Image 13 below) is in the Avery Hill archive – it is a real work of art being printed on silk with fringed edging and embroidered North monogram.

In customary style, the Colonel made sure he was the first to offer celebration of Queen Victoria's Jubilee, by holding a Ball at the Marlborough Rooms in Regent Street on Jan 21st 1887. The East London Advertiser and Tower Hamlets Independent of 5th Feb reported that it was rather too full, but was nevertheless *'the best supper we ever sat down to'.*

## Fancy Dress Ball Hotel Metropole Jan 1889

Before leaving on his final visit to Chile in 1889, the Colonel had given a farewell fancy-dress ball in January, for 800 - 1,400 guests at the Hotel Metropole by Trafalgar Square in London on 4th Jan, which was said to have cost around £8,000 (Shorney in *'Teachers in Training'* states £10,000) and included on the guest-list were Lord and Lady Randolph Churchill – with 13 peers and two Rothschilds also present. 1400 invitations had been issued but not all these were taken up, including that of the Prince of Wales. The POW, later Edward VII, had been introduced to North in 1888 by Lord Randolph Churchill (father of Winston) at a dinner given by Baron Alfred de Rothschild. North had made a gift of some shares in his latest stock flotation to the POW, as a result of which the prince had made a handsome profit, and many felt that the least he might have done in good grace, was attend the Colonel's lavish Ball. The social standing of those who deigned to accept one's invitations was a measure of the social position of the host and North aimed high with the Rothschilds, Churchills and the Prince of Wales. However, even in the last years of the 19$^{th}$ century, wealth did not entirely compensate for the accident of birth, and while the POW was happy to avail himself of the Colonel's gift of shares, he was nevertheless a stickler for etiquette and maybe not prepared to compromise his social position by accepting the dinner invitation or indeed any invitations to Avery Hill as his house visits seem to have been confined to the those comprising the upper echelons of society.

The late Victorians seem to have had a particular penchant for the Fancy Dress Ball. Here is an extract from a Guardian article in 2013 concerning New York society but it could as easily be about London:-

> *'Late 19th-century costume parties were notorious for their excess. In 1880s New York, Mrs. WK Vanderbilt's annual fancy dress balls were the talk of the town. Her 1,200 guests explored their fantasies of aristocratic heritage in costumes modelled on historical dress of the French court and British monarchy, and were so concerned with authenticity that the balls became a kind of window on history. Every minute detail of the attendees' costumes was copied from historical portraits. Guests masqueraded as Henry VII, Elizabeth I, and Marie Antoinette, among a parade of other memorable (or notorious) figures from the European past.*

*It is noteworthy that these parties took place in New York, not Paris or London. New York society was populated by people with a very short family history. The guests were people with no genuine claim to aristocratic ancestry. Emilia Müller proposes that their costumes were an attempt to justify their status. The guests sought to erase the negative connotations of a nouveau riche lifestyle, replacing them with a more respectable suggestion of lineage. By emulating European nobility, they sought to "legitimise themselves as the economic ruling class" by "buying history".[21]*

It does seem plausible that this was exactly what our Jolly Colonel had in mind when he planned his Fancy Dress Ball as he would surround himself with the trappings of lineage at his re-modelled Avery Hill; the baronial style, the motto, the coat of arms and the intertwined initials JTN everywhere in evidence.

A now corpulent North, was dressed as Henry VIII, with Mrs. North as Madame de Pompadour and their son Harry as Richelieu. Booth declared this event '*the sensation of the London winter season*', with the nitrate boom at its peak and new companies coming out almost hourly, the Colonel, he declared, would be besieged by those seeking shares, as any new issue of anything even vaguely connected to North, would be over-subscribed. The *Jovial* Colonel had managed to secure the whole of the ground and basement floors of the Metropole along with all the champagne in their cellars! For the event, the hotel was decorated with shields bearing the single letter 'N' and pages in seventeenth-century dress and a host of other servants carrying champagne and cigars, were in constant attendance as guests danced to music provided by a relay of orchestras and the band of the Colonel's own Tower Hamlets Engineers.

Celebrated caricaturist of the day, Phil May, who also happened to be a fellow son of Leeds was in attendance – May had in fact been born in New Wortley in 1864, an area adjoining Holbeck, where North himself was born. May had been a child prodigy and aged fourteen May had some of his drawings accepted by the Yorkshire Gossip newspaper, he

21   Barbara Brownie 'Victorian Socialites who used Fancy Dress to Excess' The Guardian 11th Jun 2013

did however also spend some time working in an iron foundry before moving on to pursue more artistic endeavours – sounds like he a North would have hit it off instantly, you can just imagine the congenial back-slapping between the two Yorkshiremen. May made a humorous drawing of the Norths and the Rothschilds, which he submitted to his editor at the St. Stephens Review. North had initially not been amused when he saw that a caption had been added *'Cost me £8,000 and I can't get a drink'* as though he begrudged the expenditure. However he was assured by the editor that it was exactly the opposite and indicated the extreme generosity of the host and moreover, it was absolutely true, as the usual army of free-loaders who were sure to find their way onto the guest-lists of all the Colonels lavish entertainments, had indeed drunk the Hotel Metropole dry!

The Illustrated London News of 12th January 1889 had the following account:-

*'COLONEL NORTH'S FANCY-DRESS BALL., Noteworthy among the New Year festivities in town was the magnificent Fancy-Dress Ball given by Colonel J. T. North and Mrs. North, in the sumptuous Whitehall Rooms of the Hotel Metropole, on the Fourth of January. There was a rich profusion of flowers and palms in the embellishment of the various rooms and corridors; and the liveliest dance-music was discoursed in the two ball-rooms by Lieutenant Dan Godfrey's band and the band of the Tower Hamlets Engineers. The nine hundred guests were bountifully entertained by the host and hostess, who were resplendently attired as Henry VIII. and the Duchesse de Maine (some said Madame de Pompadour), of the Louis Quinze period. Equally brilliant were the costumes of Miss North as Turkish Princess and Mr. Harry North as Duc de Richelieu, while in the garb of King Edward VI. little Master North made a picture worthy of Millais. The variety of fancy attire was remarkable. In her simple but effective robe of black, with a large diamond star in her*

*hair, Lady Randolph Churchill shone amidst the gay throng in brocaded silks and lustrous satins fashioned in every imaginable period. Lord Randolph Churchill was similarly conspicuous through the unobtrusiveness of his Court uniform as contrasted with the glowing array of huntsmen in scarlet and Mephistos in crimson, and sovereigns of all times. Besides dancing, Colonel North had provided special entertainments by Corney Grain, Professor Bertram (popular comic sketch performers at the time\*), and others ; and the supper was one of the superbest Mr. William T. Holland has ever supplied at the Metropole, the adornment of which hotel is one of the best examples, by the way, of Messrs. Maple's fine-art work. We are requested to state that the chief costumiers were Mr. B. J. Simmons, of King-Street ; M. and Madame Alias, of St. Martin's-Lane; Madame Auguste et Cie.; Messrs. Nathan, and Mrs. May.'*

\*Corney Grain performed comic songs with titles like '*The Masher King of Piccadilly*'(a *masher* being a *swell,* a *man about town)* and '*The Four Horse Sharrybang',* while Professor Bertram seems to have been a little more refined, accompanying himself on the piano performing his self-penned popular ditties.

The Canterbury Journal of 12th Jan 1889 reported:-

*'Everybody is talking of Colonel North's ball at the Hotel Metropole. It was certainly one of the most gorgeous affairs of the kind. Everybody was in fancy dress —even the band and the waiters. Colonel North was Henry VIII., Mrs. North was the Pompadour, pretty Lady Randolph, in her favourite black, suggested "Night." Lord Randolph was in Court costume, and so were good many gentlemen whose title to wear that attire was slender enough.'*

A sly poke at the *new money* pretensions of the Victorian nouveaux-riches merchants and industrialists like the Colonel.

Image 14; Jane & Emma North

## Emma's coming-of-age gala at Hotel Metropole in July 1889:-

Article from Leeds Times 5th July 1890:-

'Here stood the gallant millionaire, bravely clad in his "Tower Hamlet's" uniform; here stood Mrs. North in a most elaborate gown of green and crushed strawberry, adorned with much polychromatic embroidery; here stood young Mr. North also in a red coat; and lastly, here stood Miss Emma North, the most important personage of the evening, looking remarkably pretty in her beautifully made white gown, and wearing a most refulgent butterfly of diamonds and huge sapphires. A large table close at hand groaned beneath the weight of the many floral tributes-both baskets and bouquets which had been showered upon the young lady in honour of the day. And round this botanical centre-piece the new comers distributed themselves when their names

*had been duly announced by the heavily bearded toast-master.
But now our host has given the word of command, and the gay
crowd disperses in the direction of the two ball-rooms. Blossoms
peep out from every corner of the winding passages, and the sharp
points of innumerable palms stab one playfully as one brushes past
them. In the big saloon which looks out on to Whitehall Place red
and white are the prevailing hues: all round the walls enormous
plaques of pale petals form a background upon which the letters
J. N are traced in scarlet geraniums; thick ropes of flowers-like
magnified daisy-chains encircle the pillars in spiral coils.'*

## Children's Fancy Dress Party Jan 1891

This event was hosted by eight year-old Master Arthur North ,who
was dressed for the occasion in a handsome white satin Edward VI
costume with big sister Emma described as *'the belle of West Kent'.*[22]
Mears 'The *Cooks of Bostall',* states that Cook's children, John Oliver
Jnr (born 1881) and his sister Christian Burns (born 1884) were *invited
'because their father was Colonel North's architect'* and Mears recalls being
shown a photograph in his grandmother's (Cook's daughter?) album,
depicting the two Cook children dressed as the *Dauphin* and *Princess
Royal,* Louis XVI's children, for the occasion. Christian Burns Cook
would constantly reminisce about this party, which seems to have been
the highlight of her life. She was also in possession of two medals, one
dated 1887 and another 1889, which Mears says were always handed
out as mementoes by the Colonel at these events. Where is the 1891
medal?

Although it is easy to see the Colonel as an early incarnation of Harry
Enfield's *Loadsamoney* caricature from the 1980's Thatcher-era, he
spread his largesse far and wide and many were the beneficiaries of his
generosity and of course, he seems to have great enjoyment doing it.

---

22    The Express Jan 31st 1891

# Chapter Nine

## 'Build me a house'[23]

North and his family stayed at Southwood House, another large house just south of Avery Hill (now part of the UOG campus) as well as the Hotel Metropole, while the Avery Hill re-modelling was being carried out. Work on the house was completed in late 1890, at a final cost that some estimated to be around £200,000, although as much as £300,000 has been claimed (The Builder?). *The Nitrate Dream House* consisted of fifty rooms, including the famed Winter Garden, and a three-room Turkish Bath which must have been the finest example of its kind at the time. The *long low house* was three storeys to the east (one attic) and two to the west. The main house and stables were centrally heated (almost unheard of at the time) by a forty horse-power generator housed in a special engine room adjoining the main house. Cutler, the architect had according to the British Architect '*devised an entirely novel system of lighting*'. As the main road from Eltham to Bexley was that which ran directly in front of his property, the Colonel had managed to persuade the council to redirect this, by purchasing three acres of land at a cost of £3000 and incurring £5000 building costs, in order to accommodate the re-routed thoroughfare which is now the main Eltham to Bexley road we have today. This must have given the Colonel a real sense of self-satisfaction,

---

23    Judge Lord Coleridge in his summing up Cutler v North

to have a main thoroughfare moved at his command – that was indeed a tangible example of power and influence. With the renovations, 100 acres was also added to the estate. Edmundson mentions '*a fernery, conservatory and domed winter garden*' which doesn't really do justice to the listed Winter Garden (it warrants *capitals*) – North's *mini Crystal Palace* as many newspapers of the time dubbed it, or as The Dartford Express of 28th Sep 1889 expressed it:-

> '*Colonel North is amusing himself building an enormous residence, half barracks, half Crystal Palace at Eltham*'

The building works were not without tragedy, with that same paper in July 1889, reporting on the sad death of a young carpenter, Frederick Spicer of Jubilee Cottages (these were behind where Barclay's Bank now stands in Eltham High St.) aged 22, who fell from the roof of the picture gallery/ballroom while working on the construction. This unfortunate young man fell from a height of 50ft and was taken unconscious to The Eltham Cottage Hospital (which we now have a 21st century version of), where he was to die later that day. The newspaper account added that '*no blame was attached to the contractor*' and a verdict of '*Accidental Death*' recorded at the inquest.

Cutler's original design was for a long, two-storeyed building with two stout squareish towers, one at each end to offset the high roof of the Winter Garden, and a picture gallery/ballroom. The carriageway from the main gatehouse led to a *porte-cochére* or carriage entrance; constructed in Portland stone, it offered a pleasing contrast to the predominantly red-brick house. Above this rose the three-storeyed central section with its mansard roof and rectangular parapet crowned by a small cupola.

North's newly-acquired coat-of-arms appears on the main entrance to the house, and is repeated on four panels and a stone pediment surrounding the elaborately carved Spanish mahogany doors, with their bronze lion's heads and delicate wrought-iron grilles. On stepping through into the hallway one would have been presented with an uninterrupted view on the west side of some 500ft, through the red marble-lined sculpture gallery, picture gallery with its columns of rare Mexican onyx, to the ante-room beyond. This preponderance of stone and exotic marbles, especially if they had to travel any distance, would have added substantially to the building costs.

AVERY HILL. ELTHAM TRAINING COLLEGE FOR TEACHERS.

*Image 15; Aerial View*

## Grand Ball and Concert for the *Great and the Good* to launch refurbished Mansion Feb 1891

This event was intended to serve as North's grand opening of his newly renovated house, and he must have hoped, his first step on the ladder of his elevation to high society. A fleet of carriages would have conveyed guests from the station (what is now Mottingham, then Eltham and Mottingham on the Dartford *loop* line) to the Mansion where they dined and danced to the sounds of some of the best musicians of the time. For the occasion, the Colonel had invited the celebrated Leeds-born pianist Frederick Dawson to accompany the equally renowned Hungarian violinist Eduard Remény. Dawson was a child prodigy who by the age of ten had memorised the whole of Bach's 48 *preludes and fugues.*

The St James Gazette of 23<sup>rd</sup> Jan 1891 contained the following announcement:-

> 'REMENYI — *By kind permission and under the immediate patronage of Col. J. T. North. MONS. REMENYI, Solo Violinist to the Emperor of Austria and King of Hungary, has the honour to announce that he will give a GRAND CONCERT at CoL. NORTH's residence, Avery Hill, Eltham, Kent, to inaugurate the New Picture Gallery, on WEDNESDAY, Feb. ii, 1891, at three o'clock. Further particulars and programme will shortly be issued. Tickets at one guinea each, Mitchell's Library, Old Bond Street; Lacon and Ollier 63a, New Bond Street; and Hill and Sons, 38, New Bond Street; and at the offices of the Savoy Hotel. SPECIAL TRAIN to and from ELTHAM will be provided for ticket-holders by Col. J. T. North, leaving CHARING CROSS by South-Eastern Loop Line at two o'clock p.m'*

Tickets at 1 guinea each seems rather expensive and could this have been a charity event?

The Globe of 13<sup>th</sup> Feb reported :-

> *'At the close of the concert, those guests who remained were courteously conducted by Colonel North round the chief attractions of his house and grounds, including artificial waterfall, extensive buildings filled with palms, azaleas, and exotics in bloom, and the Louis Quinze drawing-room—a marvel of decorative art. informed us that the spacious picture gallery was intended for occasional use as a ball-room, and was less surprised than gratified to find that its acoustic qualities made it an exceptionally excellent music-room.'*

However, it would seem that Dawson disagreed as to the room's acoustic qualities, as his diary for that day states, that while the Ballroom/Picture Gallery was magnificent, it was *'a bad room for sound'* – in its defence, this room was firstly a purpose-built Picture Gallery, doubling up as a Ballroom, it was not intended to be a concert hall. The Colonel's guests would most probably have been ignorant of these acoustic deficiencies and as the packed ballroom resounded to the swishing sound of the ladies ball gowns as they waltzed the night away.

Will Robley, UOG Academic Services Librarian, had already shown, on one of his guided tours of the house, how it would have been possible for the Colonel to take his guests on a circuitous tour (*processional route*) from drawing-room, through conservatory, Winter Garden and fernery, on through the ante-room and between the sixteen huge onyx pillars supporting the minstrels gallery above, through picture and sculpture galleries and into the hallway and then back round to the drawing-room. Should the fancy have taken him, he could have taken his guest anti-clockwise by starting at the Sculpture Gallery.

On another of Will Robley's tours on Sun 25th March 2018, he used large laminated prints of photos of the Mansion from 1890/94, so we could visualise what it must have looked like as we walked around the now botched-up college interior. One could weep at the transformation! Will told us that North's Mansion was designed primarily to impress, both his contemporaries and hopefully the Prince of Wales, whom he hoped to entertain there. Entertaining had always been important, in that it offered an opportunity to attract a suitable match for one's marriageable children. Perhaps the Colonel thought some impoverished member of the aristocracy may be tempted by the reputedly enormous dowry that was likely to be settled on Emma, this being carefully weighed against any potential suitor's pedigree. As Nancy Mitford's character Lady Stanley observes in '*The Stanleys of Alderley*' :- '*Half the peerage have no grandfathers*'.

Will talked us through the arrival of a typical guest to a North *entertainment* and how he would be perambulated round the house on a tour guaranteed to impress. His carriage would be met in the porte-cochére by a liveried North footman and he would be conveyed to the entrance hall, where his hosts awaited. His coat would be taken by servants and the Colonel and Mrs North would guide him on a processional route through their house, which had been planned in detail to take in all the wonder and magnificence of their new abode. First through the Sculpture Gallery, where one was expected to show one's knowledge of classical Greek and Roman antiquity – not sure how the Colonel would manage this, with humour, I would imagine – he was not for false airs and graces and I am sure would be the first to admit of the gaps in his knowledge. The guest would then be presented with the awe-inspiring spectacle of the magnificent Picture Gallery/Ballroom with its walls almost completely covered with pictures, some measuring 30ftx20ft and with such titles as '*Massacre of the Innocents*'. Again, one cannot guess as to whether the Colonel was a real art lover, but anecdotal evidence seems to point at his buying pieces for their size maybe, rather than their artistic merit. However, guests could not but be impressed at such a room, with its green onyx doorways, pillars and minstrels gallery, and all lit by the latest electric arc-light chandeliers. One would proceed under the 16 onyx pillars into the ante-room behind which one could pause to reflect, and looking back, be presented with the un-interrupted vista back through the Picture Gallery and beyond the Sculpture Gallery to the Entrance Hall. Your tour would then proceed through the three glass-houses - the three separate houses being referred to individually as the *fernery* and the *conservatory*, with the larger middle one referred to as the Winter Garden. It was only after the Colonel's time that the *whole* was referred to as the Winter Garden. One could marvel at the many exotic plants and trees, many of which our host had brought back with him from Chile – the Colonel would be able to regale his guests with tales of his sojourn in tropical climes, which again could not fail to impress as many of his guests would probably not have set foot beyond their home county. We could then marvel at the delicate Fernery and beyond it the mini *Crystal Palace* of the Winter Garden proper, with its array of cacti and palms reaching to the 100ft high dome. Then lastly on to the peaceful Conservatory with its goldfish pond and the voluptuous recumbent marble figure of Galatea in the middle. Then up the steps and through the double-doors and into the Drawing Room where cocktails await. And, should fulsome praise of the delights that had been witnessed was not forthcoming, then the Colonel would have every right not to repeat his invitation!

While being at the forefront of the late-Victorian *nouveaux-riches* palaces in the greater London area, the Mansion was not generally considered a building of great architectural merit, although no expense had been spared in the decoration and fitting of the interior. Jill Franklin in '*The Country House*', states that by this time the emphasis in country house design went from *aesthetic* to *comfort* and with the expansion of the railway, businessmen like North, found that they might combine the pleasure of country living with ease of commuting to their place of business in the City. A. Hunting in his dissertation on Avery Hill for Thames Polytechnic Faculty of Architecture in 1977 had said the house had '*all the trappings of the nouveaux-riches of the period, above all conservatories and electric light*'. The focus was now on the treatment of the interior of the house rather than its architectural appeal, and in this respect, Avery Hill did not disappoint.

Franklin contrasts the original landed gentry and the *nouveaux riches* industrial entrepreneurs (like North) and the snobbery displayed in publications like the *Architect* in 1873 (you can almost hear the sneer):- '*when a self-made warehouseman of Leadenhall Street or attorney of Chancery Lane....builds his country house and farms a hundred acres in Kent...the chances are that it is not a country house at all, but a suburban villa out of place*'.

Alas, while this new money might purchase the trappings of country-house life, the status and social position conferred by the lineage of a landed estate, still remained beyond their grasp.

The Architectural Association said of the Colonel's new house;- '*The general character of the house is more remarkable for the large sums of money expended than for its high artistic result*'. T. Raffles Davison thought otherwise, in his '*Avery Hill Rambling Sketches No 710*' which appeared in *The British Artchitect* of Jan 3rd 1890, he enthuses that the Colonel '*had erected one of the finest modern houses in this country*'. Similarly, *The Dartford Express* in Aug 1890 ventures:- '*Colonel North's new residence, which might well be describes as New Eltham Palace, is now quite complete*'.

English Heritage may wax lyrical of the modern conveniences of Eltham Palace as installed by the Courtaulds (like their central vacuum-cleaning system), but North's innovations at Avery Hill were much more adventurous (let's face it he was an *engineer*) and his house pre-dates Eltham Palace by some 40+ years.

It is odd that Arthur North was the only member of the family in residence at Avery Hill for the 1891 Census, along with three female relatives staying; Mary Emma Beasley, North's niece, being his sister Emma's daughter, and her daughters Beatrice and Naomi Beasley (or Beazley?). Mary Emma Beasley, also had a son Mavin John who had been born in 1884 in Iquique, she had divorced her husband Arthur William John Beasley in 1891 and taken up residence with her children at her uncle's house in Avery Hill. In addition there was a housekeeper, dressmaker and eleven domestic servants of whom two were men. With the exception of one girl aged 17, all were in their twenties and thirties.

The census also lists as living in the Stables; the coachman, his wife and two grown-up sons who were both grooms, in addition the mother-in-law and two boarders who were also grooms. One of the lodges housed the gardener and his wife, the other was occupied by the lodge-keeper and his wife.

Where was the Colonel and the rest of the family? Maybe he was visiting at another country house along with his butler/footmen as was the habit at that time.

# Chapter Ten

## The Mansion

### West Gateway Entrance and Lodge

To most visitors, this would have been the first glimpse of the house as this was the main entrance from the newly-constructed Bexley Road and was that used by most non-trade visitors to Avery Hill. The structure is grand even by North's standards, but this was the entrance which he intended would be used by the Prince of Wales, whom he hoped to one day entertain

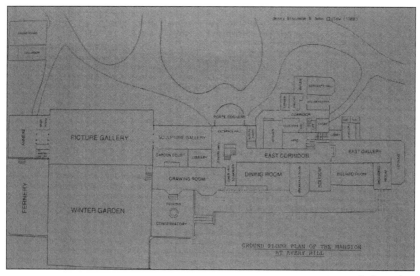

Image 16; Ground Floor Plan

at Avery Hill. Sadly, the hoped for honour of a visit by the Prince did not happen, but the Duke of Cambridge, who was reputed to have been a possible match for the prince's mother, Queen Victoria prior to Albert's appearance, was reputedly entertained at Avery Hill on more than one occasion and it was also rumoured when the house was up for sale in 1898 that the Duke of York might be considering purchasing. Prince George Duke of York had become second in line to the English throne following the tragic death of his elder brother Prince Albert of pneumonia in 1892. Maybe he saw it as a potential country retreat but still within the London boundaries.

In order to achieve maximum impact, Cutler was careful to subordinate the adjoining lodge to the entrance by making the arched gateway taller than the lodge. The gateway was constructed of red brick with its molding and crest delicately carved out of the brickwork. The roof of the gateway is vaulted in brick with matching brown-red roof-tiles. Apparently, there was *oak block paving* on the roadway below the arch which does not seem very functional as it was open to the elements.

North's adopted motto *Animo et Fide* (with courage and faith, and which coincidentally is my ancestor's motto also), is found on the brickwork above the main gatehouse and the large wrought-iron gates feature North's initials *JTN,* intertwined. Wrought iron-work was by Messrs. Richardson, Ellson and Co of Holborn. All the moldings, arms and enrichments are of *cut brickwork.* The lodge consisted of living-room, kitchen, scullery, pantry, china- closet and coal place, with three bedrooms overhead – this was home to the lodge-keeper and his family.

The total cost of construction of the gateway and lodge was £2,500, which we are told would have purchased at the time a fair number of houses or paid the annual salaries of some 20-25 teachers in 1890![24]

The smaller lodge to the east (facing onto Avery Hill Rd), was home to the gardener and his family - this entrance was for the use of tradesmen

24    A. Hunting 'Avery Hill and It's Winter Garden' Dissertation to Thames Polytechnic Faculty of Architecture Dec 1977

and other less-exalted guests and for anything too tall to negotiate the main arched gateway. Palm trees for the Winter Garden and 30ft by 20ft canvases destined for the Picture Gallery spring to mind.

### Porte-Cochére / Entrance

Image 17; Front Entrance - Then & Now

Guests carriages, having passed through the main gateway, would proceed to the main entrance under a *porte-cochére* or carriage entrance, where visitors would disembark to be met, probably by one of the North footmen who would announce your arrival while your coachman took your carriage around to the stables. Raffles-Davison of The British Architect reports:-

> *'The first thing one has to do in some houses is to find the front doorway, here it is emphatic and inviting'*

The *porte-cochére* was constructed of Portland stone which contrasted well with the predominantly red-brick structure of the rest of the house, with its columns and balustrade serving to draw one's eye upwards to the high mansard roof topped by a parapet and small cupola. The elaborately carved Spanish mahogany entrance doors were reputed to have been destined for Lima Cathedral but were the wrong size, which is plausible as the Cathedral was undergoing extensive renovations at the same time as the Avery Hill building works. Russell's account of the final visit to Chile in 1889 describes their party visiting the Cathedral so it is quite plausible that they returned with the doors. The wrought iron grilles on either side of the doors were cast by Messrs, Richardson, Ellson & Co, who were responsible for most of the ironwork around the mansion.

The newly-acquired North coat-of-arms is repeated on the main entrance to the house, on four panels and a stone pediment surrounding the entrance doors, which feature an eagle with '*1890*' beneath it's feet. Frances Consitt a pupil in the early days of the ladies college, recalls in her reminiscences in the college magazine that there were large brass lion's heads in the middle of each door, one had disappeared during the war and the other could be seen in the Art room, in the early college days.[25] These lion's head's had been modelled by Monsieur Aumonier and cast by M. Buhree at his Merton studio.

---

25    'Jottings on the College Buildings and Early Years of the College' Avery Hill Reporter July 1949 Frances Consitt

The Front Entrance has survived relatively unscathed but a glance at Image 17 above, shows where everything to the left of the entrance was demolished in 1947, to be replaced by unsympathetic educational structures.

**Entrance Hall**

On passing through the main entrance, (where sadly the intricate mosaic flooring is being damaged by the excessive student footfall), one entered an inner Entrance Hall, paved in marble, with directly opposite, ornately-carved double doors of Spanish mahogany, again carved by Monsieur Aumonier, who seems to have been responsible for most of the wood-carving in the house. The carving on these doors is particularly fine, again depicting the newly-acquired North coat-of-arms, with *lions rampant* and winged cherubs surrounding a shield with two chevrons and three stars, with the motto *Animo et Fide* beneath. It was mooted that North had used the star as depicted on the Chilean flag. These double doors hid a shallow cloaks-cupboard, inside which it is still possible to see the outline of the steps of the Marble Staircase which can be seen running up on the left towards the First Floor Corridor.

Above the mahogany panelling, a coved frieze depicting warriors and crests surrounding. Cabinet work of *Australian padaux wood* (similar to rosewood). There is a glazed dome above, giving light to what otherwise would have been a very gloomy space, and an elaborate carved chimneypiece, with classical figures and *pre-Raphaelite* style tiles. Booth in 'Palmy Days,' mentions a huge stuffed bear in the entrance hall, with a silver salver on which guests would drop their calling cards. There are photos showing this bear and also a complete bear-skin rug on the floor and stags-head trophy on the wall. The stuffed bear, a 4ft 6" tall *curious bronze figure of a Chinese warrior on horseback* and a Japanese suit of armour on a stand, are listed in the Wilkinson auction catalogue of the Mansion contents in 1898, as having come from the Entrance Hall.

Beyond this was another smaller inner hall to the left which was concealed from the main entrance by an elaborately carved screen which hid from view a cloak and hat cupboard, very handy for the hats and coats of both the family and any guests, thus keeping the hallway uncluttered.

This inner hallway gave access to both the principal ground floor apartments and the first-floor bedrooms via the exquisite white marble staircase on the right, while straight ahead was another hallway, described as the *central hall* which survives intact with exquisite mosaic flooring and this leads to the Drawing Room.

Frances Consitt's memoir, tells us that Italian workers were employed in the laying of the mosaic floors of the corridors (some of which can still be seen in the entrance hall and corridor to the Drawing Room), the carved wood-work, graceful iron-work and stucco ceilings. She tells us that the two recurring motifs in the decoration are the *shell* of the *Pilgrim Shell* (signifying a higher loyalty) and the *English rose*. Colonel North's adopted motto of *animo et fide* (strength and courage) was incorporated into the college crest as it was deemed to be equally appropriate for an educational establishment.

## Library

To the right of the Entrance Hall and just off the left side of the Sculpture Gallery. The Colonel was so taken with this octagonal room of the original house, that he insisted it be worked into the new building and luckily, it seems to have survived almost exactly as it was with all the fitted carved walnut and pine bookcases intact and the most striking green Sicilian marble fireplace. The '*Celebrity at Home*' article mentions '*a French garniture de cheminée, which takes the form of a steam-hammer and plate-rollers, surrounded by a score of glittering specimens of silver ore from Huantajaya*'. It is not hard to see how such an *objet,* of a kind much beloved of the Victorians, would have appealed to the engineer in North.

Will Robley explained how the door into this room from the Sculpture Gallery replaced a window from the original house. He also pointed out where a new bookcase has replaced what would have been a door into the Drawing Room, which was in fact two separate rooms in the original house – he had establish this as the original bookcases were of veneered wood, whereas this new addition was stained wood.

Edmundson mentions two full-size portraits of Jane and Emma North (See Image 14 below) by Philip Tennyson, which I believe were returned to North family descendants.

It is difficult to establish exactly how much of the original house formed part of the new, as Cutler's brief, as detailed in a short note from North dated 1st Fab 1889, was for 'additions and alterations', and not, apparently, for a new house. Only parts of the Drawing Room and the Library have been described as being part of the original house, if that is the case most of the original house would in fact have been demolished. T. Raffles Davison in his Rambling Sketches No 710, describing the newly remodeled house says:- 'some of the rooms are old; the library is entirely so and the drawing-room partially'.

Unfortunately the UOG currently use this room for meeting, so consequently, most of the space is taken up with a large modern table and chairs which very much spoils the effect.

Maybe the Colonel inherited the Library ready-stocked with books as the Wilkinson's Auction catalogue lists Cicero, Milton, Shakespeare, Scott, Tennyson along with additions easily recognisable as the Colonels own contribution:- Kennel Club Calendar 1889-93, Mr. Spong's Sporting Tour and ten copies of William Howard Russell's 1889 account of their final trip to Chile 'A Visit to Chile...' ready to be handed out to any of those doubters who might question the nature of his nitrate businesses.

## Sculpture Gallery

It was reading a description of this impressive structure that first spurred my interest in the Mansion, as like most Eltham residents I was oblivious to the very existence of the magnificent remaining parts of the North house. This room is still relatively intact – the red marble paneled walls with twenty small stained-glass windows (now missing) above and ornate geometric design marble floor. Photographs of 1890, show the sculpture gallery lined on both sides with pedestals with mainly busts atop. Those of the Colonel and Mrs. North by Raemackers from 1887, which once faced each other across the middle of the sculpture gallery and subsequently in the senior common-room (Drawing Room) have now been returned to living family members in Wales, as the UOG prepares to vacate the Mansion (Apr 2020). A walk through the Sculpture Gallery would have given the Colonel's guests the opportunity to hopefully, dazzle with their knowledge of classical antiquity.

Shorney refers to the *'Marble Hall'* which I believe refers to the Sculpture Gallery, being used as a gymnasium and that this was highly unsatisfactory due to its stone floor and poor ventilation making it

Image 18; Sculpture Gallery

123

unsuitable for physical exercise. The LCC minutes of meetings from 1903/4, mention that the roof of the Sculpture Gallery was flat and constructed with iron girders covered with cement and as the iron girders were liable to expansion in hot weather, the cement had cracked resulting in water incursion. Various remedies had been adopted but to no avail. The proposal was that between £55 to £65 be spent by the Council on asphalting the roof and this was accepted by.

Wilkinson's auction catalogue of 1896 lists these items, amongst the many coming from the Sculpture Gallery:-

*5ft marble/bronze group 'Pierrot and Beggar' by Calvi of Milan*

*Marble bust of Grace Darling by J.A. Raemackers 1888 on onyx pedestal*

*Marble bust of Napoleon by Chaudel*

*Italian Marble Group 4ft4" tall 'Girl Swinging a Boy'*

*A Sumptuously Designed Historical State Chair with carved gilt frame, surmounted by an Imperial Crown with Napoleon's Coat of Arms with photograph and history of the chair in a plush frame*

## Garden Court

Will Robley of UOG, maintains that this room came about as a result of the necessity of retaining the original Library and Drawing Room. Accessible from both the Library and the Picture Gallery, the Garden Court was an enclosed, two storey open-roofed, small courtyard with garden and fountain, completely tiled in Burmantofts (yellow tiles with coloured frieze), with flooring of Minton tiles. When I mentioned my particular interest in the Turkish Bath, Clara at UOG had taken me to the Quiet Study room, which covers the area where the Garden Court stood and pointed towards the ceiling which had some glass panels through which we could see a border of some yellowish ceramic (Minton) tiles – she seemed to think these might be remnants of the Turkish Bath but they must be from the ceiling-level first floor section of the Garden Court – the Turkish Bath was behind this on the first floor (garden side). Alison Goss an archivist at UOG had made the same observation to Malcolm Shifrin, author of victorianturkishbaths. org.uk and *Victorian Turkish Baths* (the book), in a letter of 18th Apr 1996. Having re-read the account of the Turkish Bath in The Builder, it seems to suggest an arched window which overlooked this courtyard from the first floor and Will Robley suggests maybe staircase access from the north end of Turkish Bath. More recently, Will showed an even better view of the remaining tiling of the Garden Court, through the windows that run along the top of the Sculpture Gallery.

Also a small hallway from Garden Court running behind the Drawing Room with steps down to the Conservatory on the right.

### Picture Gallery / Ballroom

This room would have been the '*jewel in the crown*' of North's Mansion and we are lucky that it has survived relatively unscathed, despite superficial alterations for its use as a library during UOG's tenure. Jill Franklin mentions *The Architect* in 1872, lamenting the rarity of ballrooms and picture galleries in country houses of the time as a result of the fashion for reduction in the number of reception rooms. However, Avery Hill was designed with entertaining in mind along with maximum ostentatious *showiness*. Having recently visited the Wallace Collection and Dulwich Picture Gallery, in my opinion, Avery Hill's gallery is far superior to the main galleries in both of these.

T.Raffles Davison of the British Architect writes in his 1890 *Rambling Sketches No 710 'Avery Hill'*:-

> '*The picture gallery is probably the finest in effect which my readers will have ever seen*'

The Colonel had started to collect both paintings and sculpture even before he embarked on the house remodeling and he now had a spectacular one hundred by fifty feet room with a forty four feet high ceiling in which to display his acquisitions for the delight of all comers. The picture gallery was purpose-built and therefore had no windows, being lit from above through a glass ceiling or *clerestory*, an architectural term, describing a high section of wall that contains windows above

Image 19; Picture Gallery - Then & Now

eye level. The purpose is to admit light, fresh air, or both, without light focusing directly on the picture-hung walls, which would have been damaging for the delicate canvases. This was, according to T. Raffles Davison of the *British Architect* 1890, superior to any '*top light*' he had seen and he also observes the 27ft high walls designed to accommodate the largest pictures (and the Colonel liked *large*). He also notes that 70 tons of iron had been used in the construction of the roof. The walls were covered in embossed crimson silk-velvet with a dado of *verde antique*, a highly polished dark green marble-like stone with white veining, which would have contrasted well against the green onyx of the 16 columns and minstrel's gallery.

The Colonel had already purchased the whole of Italian artist Sciuti's collection as shown at the Italian Exhibition in 1888, for £10,000. North had supposedly told a Primrose League (gardening association) deputation to Avery Hill in September 1890:- '*I bought these pictures and had to build the palace to put them in*'. One canvas, '*Massacre of the Innocents*' was reputedly 30ftx20ft, with '*The Silver King*' being another of the larger pictures. He had also acquired a *moral story* series of paintings by popular Victorian artist William Powell Frith which sounds much in the same genre as Hogarth's *Progress* series, so it is not surprising to find that Frith was described as being '*the greatest British painter of the social scene since Hogarth*'. Frith was also for '*The Derby Day*' executed 1856-8, which most readers are probably familiar with even without knowing the artist. While visiting a gallery in St. James's (2019), I stumbled across one of Frith's most famous paintings '*A Private View at the Royal Academy*', painted in 1881 and showing a crowd gathered in the gallery, including many Victorian notables, philanthropist Baroness Burdett-Coutts (of the banking family), politicians and celebrities of the time like Oscar Wilde and the actress Ellen Terry to name just a few. The gallery owner said this was the first time the picture was up for sale since it had been bought at the Royal Academy – we were told it had come from a country house and it came with a £10 million pound price-tag!

The Bradford Daily Telegraph of 13th Oct 1890 was effusive in its praise of the Colonel's new house;-

> *'The visitor turned adrift in the vast house may well imagine himself the hero of an Arabian Nights Tale as he wanders from one dream of loveliness to another. I don't suppose, even in one of the Royal Palaces, there is a ballroom which in dimensions, fittings and decoration, can eclipse that of Colonel North's.'*

The author does however question the Colonel's choice of artwork for his *'hall of mirth and pleasure'*, with Frith's *'Road to Ruin'* not necessarily what one might want to see as one indulged in the Colonel's hospitality!

There were also life-size statues of Garibaldi, Lord Palmerston and Count Cavour by Giovanni Pandiani and various other marble and terra-cotta statuary along with epic canvases by Richard Caton Woodville II – *The Charge of the Light Brigade, The Relief of Lucknow and Blenheim* and a newspaper article mentions his *comely North African matron,* although I can't locate the picture he refers to. Other British painters represented in the Picture Gallery were William Walter Ouless and Frederick Goodall's *'Neither do I condemn thee'* and *'Misery and Mercy'* and pictures of a *sporting* nature like Sturgis' *'Jem Selby's Drive to Brighton'*. These artists were all very popular in Victorian times but have since fallen out of favour, as has much of Victorian decorative art.

Side by side with the *horse and hound* pictures, were some large naval scenes, Dutch religious subjects and a large portrait of Randolph Churchill (by a Mr. Neumann) - a bit sycophantic!!.

One of the centre-pieces of the gallery was the American artist Albert Bierstadt's *The Last of the Buffalo,* a large canvas measuring six feet by ten feet. It could almost be this that is the subject of the following anecdote in Mrs. George Cornwallis West's *'The Reminiscences of Lady Randolph Churchill'* of 1908:-

*'Dining with us once, I was much amused at the description (Colonel North) gave me of his picture gallery. That very day he had bought a 'grand picture' for which he had given the large sum of £8,000. I asked who it was by; that he could not remember, nor even the subject, 'But,' he added, 'It is twelve feet by eight!' He was a kindly man, and very charitable.'*

In the *'King of Avery Hill'*, from Leeds Archives, the writer says North paid $15,000 (£3000 at that time) for *The Last of the Buffalo*. While going through the UOG archives, I came across correspondence from an American art historian, Dr. Gerald Carr, who was in the process of writing *'Bierstadt's West'* and he was asking whether there were any photographs of the Picture Gallery showing *'The Last of The Buffalo'* in situ, which sadly, there were not.

Another amusing anecdote in *'Stories of Colonel North'* in The Leeds Mercury of May 16th 1896:- North, although fond of pictures, hated what one would call *'doing galleries'*. Once being pressed to go and see a picture *'after Rubens'*, he quickly replied *'After Rubens! Why, surely Rubens was the brute they were after last year when you dragged me in here. Haven't they caught the old cuss yet?'*. We know that the popular press liked to poke fun at North's lack of *sophistication*, but on occasions like this he was more likely to be playing to the gallery, or this might just be one of the many *tongue-in-cheek* stories concocted by playful journalists, like Binstead and Booth of the Sporting Times, for the delectation of their *laddish* readership. North, being of the sporting fraternity, would almost definitely have been a regular reader as well as being a popular subject of *The Sporting Times*, or *Pink 'Un'* as it was affectionately known due to its being printed on pink paper. This name had stuck after a newsagent asked a customer what he would like and he replied *'I'll 'ave the pink 'un'*.

At the auction held at Avery Hill on March 21st 1898, after the Colonel's death, it was reported by The Times that many of North's prized pictures were sold at knock-down prices. The Sciuti paintings were sold for fractions of what the Colonel had originally paid. Bierstadt's magnificent '*Last of the Buffalo*' went for a derisory ninety-five guineas. It was a painful occasion for those living artists to see their work demeaned in this manner.

A satirical sketch at the time quotes Lord Tennyson's hero in *The Palace of Art* '*I built my soul a lordly pleasure-house, Wherein at ease for aye to dwell*' - it goes on to compare North to this hero with his '*elaborate and fastidious instructions as to the details of his Picture Gallery, the Colonel ordering 'mammoth canvases by the square – yard, almost by the acre!*'

The British Architect of 6ᵗʰ Sep 1889 talks of:- '*the best looms in France are busily engaged in producing the thousands of yards of crimson silk velvet for the adornment of the ballroom*' .

We have to assume they are referring to the walls, as there are no windows as such, other than the *clerestory* top-lighting in this space.

The Picture Gallery doubled as a ballroom on those many occasions when the North's put on their famously lavish entertainments at Avery Hill. Although its main purpose was as a gallery, there was always the intention that it should double-up for entertainments like concerts/balls. Why else would you have built in such a lavish onyx Minstrels Gallery?

In the early college years, this room was used as both an assembly and dining room, as well as for music lessons, and sadly, the college proprietors perhaps feeling that the crimson tapestry wallcovering was not suitably sober, had it removed. As for the music lessons, the room was found not to be conducive to music-making, much as Frederick Dawson, the Colonels virtuoso pianist and fellow Leeds-man, had found in 1891. Due to its multi-functionality, the continual re-arranging of chairs and tables was found most tiresome for the ladies of the college.

In 1910 a gymnasium was erected alongside the Ballroom/Picture Gallery and even though the construction is sympathetic to the original house being in red brick, it still totally obscures the view of the house proper, as one approaches from the main gateway.

## Minstrels Gallery

Constructed in rare Mexican onyx, the Minstrels Gallery was considered the finest example of such a feature, in the world and understandably so – not even the greatest of great houses could boast such a magnificent structure. Worked by P. Trollope and Sons at a cost of £3,000. During UOG's tenure, members of staff were warned not to use the minstrel's gallery for any tete-a-tete, as the acoustics were so good even a whisper was audible at the other end of the gallery. Apparently there had been a a frieze above the minstrel's gallery depicting nymphs in a state of undress and this was painted over in 1908 when the house became a ladies college, in order to spare the young ladies blushes. So what had been deemed acceptable for the stuffy Victorian matriarchs was then unacceptable to the enlightened young things of the Edwardian era?

 This balcony was the location for the Avery Hill archive when I was researching and I was lucky enough to be able to view the whole room from this *crows-nest,* imagining I was looking down on a room-full of the Colonels guest's with one of his famous entertainments in full swing.

Passing under the sixteen onyx columns beneath the Minstrels Gallery, led into the:-

## Ante-Room/Annexe/*Conservatory*

This room does not seem to have had any formal function other than giving easy access round to the Winter Garden, which would have been essential when the Colonel gave visitors his circular tour, plus the uninterrupted 500ft view through to the vinery from the Entrance

Hall. It would also be where musicians could gather prior to climbing up to the Minstrel's Gallery. Because of its good light it was used for art classes during the college years, however the glass roof presented enormous problems turning the room into a greenhouse in summer and a refrigerator in winter

## Winter Garden

Winter Gardens were another Victorian innovation, giving the opportunity to stroll in pleasant surroundings in any weather – the English garden was renowned but due to inclement weather, not

*Image 20; Winter Garden*

very functional outside the summer months. Jill Franklin writing of Avery Hill in 1981 says;- '*once filled with rare plants brought from South America, is still lavishly maintained, though most of the house is gone*'. Of course it ceased to be even adequately maintained once responsibility became UOG's. Franklin also adds '*outsized winter gardens had always seemed a trifle vulgar and by the end of the century (19th), iron and glass conservatories went right out of fashion*'. Having waxed lyrical regarding Avery Hill Winter Garden, why did Franklin not include a photograph, when the ones she does include, look far inferior?

Total building costs for this *mini Crystal Palace* were £60,000, £6000 for the glass alone; that is £20,000 more than the Colonel had originally intended for the *entire* house re-modelling! Jill Franklin claims that many grand houses of that time were constructed for less than £50,000. T. Raffles Davison tells us that 150 tons of iron was used in the construction. Shorney mentions that there were rumours in 1912, that the Parks and Open Spaces Committee were contemplating demolishing the conservatories and Winter Garden which had proved so expensive to maintain (they must have retained responsibility for upkeep during College tenure?). It is telling that Hampton's auction catalogue of 1901 does not include a photograph of the Winter Garden, although it does for the Fernery and Conservatory, so perhaps after five years of neglect it may have been looking the worse for wear by this time. Ironwork falling from the roof prompted closure in 1912, but following a petition organised by a Mr. Squires, who collected 5,000 signatures, and after the Parks Committee had spent £2,750 on repairs, the Winter Garden was re-opened to the public in 1913. However, following damage in WW2, the garden was not opened again to the public until 1962, after renovations costing £18,000. The architect employed on this occasion was criticised for destroying much of the garden's Victorian character by removing the rockeries (stone landscaping), waterfalls of the Fernery and the marble staircase from the Conservatory to/from the Drawing Room.

The Winter Garden, while being the *jewel in the crown,* was at the same time, the *albatross round the neck* of Avery Hill due to exorbitant maintenance costs and costs/responsibilty still remains a contentious issue.

There are actually three structures that comprise what we now refer to as the Winter Garden:-

## The Fernery

Dimensions mirroring those of the Conservatory (45ft x 45ft x 40ft high). Accessed via the garden terrace and with steps/doors leading to/ from the *Annexe* behind the Picture Gallery. I think I have seen photos showing a rockery with low-level planting in contrast to the tall palms of the adjoining Winter Garden. Wilkinson catalogue mentions '*rockwork arches, waterfall* and *miniature lake – The whole most tastefully arranged and planted with a collection of palms, ferns and water-lilies'.* As stated above, much of the character here was removed by the unsympathetic makeover given in 1962.

## The Winter Garden

This was actually the main central structure measuring 100ft x 100ft with 90ft high roof – one of its functions being to hide the windowless, box-like structure of the Picture Gallery from the garden aspect. Access was both from a set of steps via the Conservatory and from the garden terrace. A statue of Mercury still survives on the top of the central dome of the Winter Garden. The original lush planting has mostly disappeared although a few bedraggled looking palm trees survive. There is an intricate mechanical system of both watering and ventilation in evidence and both looking in need of urgent attention. I have been told that Avery Hill Winter Garden constructed as it is with 25ft+ arched walls of red brick would therefore not strictly be considered a *glasshouse* or a rival for Kew, which was built entirely of glass – *the world's largest glasshouse.*

## The Conservatory

Access to this was from both the Drawing Room and from the garden terrace. It measures 45ft x 45ft with 40ft high roof. A marble statue by Ansiglione of *Galatea* reclining on a dolphin, can still be seen in the centre of the goldfish pond. In the '*Reminiscences of Dorothy Franklin*' 1907-1909, remembering her time as a student during the Mansion's time as a ladies teacher-training college, she writes '*Art was taught in the Conservatory. This was about the only place where one got a glimpse of the outside world, and that strange phenomenon known as 'man'. Hence work was inclined to be punctuated by 'Look, quick there's a man!* This reminds me of my time as a convent girl at Notre Dame Girls School in Southwark in the 1960's – we had no playground and during breaks, we had to walk in columns across St George's Rd to the park next to the Imperial War Museum, where we could cast furtive glances at passing *boys*.

Continuing on the Colonel's circular tour, guests could mount the steps giving access to:-

## Drawing Room

Small mosaic-floored (one of the few sections to have survived intact) hallway from main entrance hallway leading to the ivory-inlaid door to this lovely room, 60ft in length and during North's time, with spectacular views across parkland to the south and with access to both the Winter Garden and Garden Court. This room would originally have had the walls panelled in green and gold brocaded satin.

Raffles Davison[26] suggests that some of the drawing room might have formed part of the original Boyd house, like the library – Will Robley confirms that the doors at the far end are original to the Regency house. There are figures carved into the brick on the doorway with steps leading

---

26    T. *Raffles Davison 'The British Architect'* 1890

onto the Conservatory. Wilkinson's Contents Sales Catalogue of 1898 lists many exquisitely carved ivory figures as coming from the Drawing Room.

This room was utilised as the College's first Library and managed to retain its handsome mirrors and gold tapestries during that period – were the proprietors not worried that their young ladies might spend too much time basking in their own reflections rather than poring over dusty tomes? Students got in the habit of taking their needlework or knitting with them into the Library but this practice was frowned upon by the teachers as being too frivolous for such august surroundings and the needlewomen were banished to the Eastern Common Room (Lounge). The Drawing Room was subsequently used as a Senior Common Room by the ladies college and is still used as a Common Room by the UOG (2019).

**Eastern Wing (all demolished in 1947 except Lavatory):-**

**East Corridor**

To the left of the main entrance hall, an oak paneled corridor 90ft long and 12 ft wide gave access to a series of majestically appointed rooms - on the right;-

**Dining Room**

50ft long with all-round, magnificently carved cabinetry for the display of the North family's prized porcelain and plate. The mantle and molded jambs and frieze supporting the mantle in Verona yellow marble. Paneled throughout in finely carved Spanish mahogany worked by Monsieur Aumonier, who seems to have been responsible for most of the other wood carving in the house, on doors, entrance hall etc.

We know that the Colonel often had 20-30 guests to Sunday lunch, so it is likely that he had a comparable number to dinner on occasions. Everyone would congregate in the Drawing Room and when dinner was announced, the host would offer his arm to the pre-eminent lady present, while the rest of the party lined up behind them – the party would then process to the Dining Room. In the design of country houses it was therefore desirable that there should be some distance between drawing and dining rooms, in order to add some pomp and ceremony to the proceedings. Avery Hill was ideal as this process would have given guests an opportunity to catch a glimpse of the magnificent white marble staircase and the lavishly appointed corridor leading to the Dining Room.

Three pairs of French windows opening on to the verandah and grounds.

**Breakfast Room**

Small but luxuriously finished in silk damask, the breakfast room would be utilised on those mornings following a grand dinner in the dining room, meaning that the servants would not have to stay up until guests had finished, in order to clear away the table for the following morning. Housemaids and kitchen maids toiled invisibly in the wings, while the liveried footmen would have been very much on display.

This room may also have been where the North family took their meals when they were not entertaining guests.

**Boudoir**

This room was designated a lady's *evening sitting room*, and was separate from her morning and dressing rooms and was probably where Mrs. North and the female guests retired to after dinner, while the male guests followed the Colonel to the nearby Billiard Room, for whisky, cigars and raucous male banter, away from the delicate ears of the ladies. This was the female equivalent of the male *study* and male guests would not normally enter unless invited. With its feminine touches, such as the velvet dado and silk paneled walls and like all the other rooms, an intricately molded plaster ceiling, There would have been much Victorian *frippery*, with lots of small tables laden with trinkets and *objets*.

The area to the left of the East Corridor had a large number of service rooms including the Kitchen, scullery, larder, pantry, servant's quarters and various storerooms.

**Visitors Staircase (left off the Eastern Corridor)**

I had not heard of this until I came across Cutler's drawing as featured in *The Builder* of September 30 1893 (below). I understand this staircase was to the left of the Eastern Corridor.

*At the far end of the oak-panelled corridor were a set of five Sienna/Verona yellow marble steps down to the;-*

Image 22; Visitors Staircase

Image 23; Eastern/Renaissance Gallery

## Eastern/Renaissance Gallery

This was actually another hall, 58ft in length by 20ft wide, the walls of which were exquisitely paneled in walnut covered in *Tyne Castle tapestry*, some accounts say this is a type of damask, but looks to be more like a tooled and embossed leather, a process perfected in Scotland, this was worked in two shades of gold (*See Additional Information*). The ornate flooring worked in *Pompeiian mosaics*, the lamp fittings and the ornate plaster ceilings were features common throughout much of the house. Above the tapestry wall panels ran a border of small semi-circular stained glass windows enclosing portraits of well-known artists. This gallery was known as the *Fountain Corridor* during its early days as a training college and this was the '*splendor and opulence staff and students enjoyed in the first three decades of the college's history*'.[27] Wilkinson's Auction Catalogue of 1898 lists a most interesting piece as having come from a cabinet in this Gallery, *a compressed human head* – the Colonel picked up some strange mementoes during his sojourn in South America. Off this gallery were the doors to the Billiard Room and Morning Room to the right and on the left side, the door to a cloak-room and the celebrated *Lavatory*, while running along the end of the gallery, with views facing eastwards, was a Lounge.

## Billiard Room

A 40ft room, lit from the sides by electric lighting and not with the usual *top light*. The striking colours of the walls, lined in slabs of *Numidian yellow* marble, pink *pavonazzo* relieved with *verde antique,* between which were double pilasters of *Numidian yellow*. Panels, architraves and chimney-piece in *Numidian yellow* marble with the pilasters, caps and cornices of Verona yellow marble and margins (borders?) of *Lissoughton green*. Raffles Davison mentions that this room was executed by Mr. Chappell, the main contractor for the building and a Mr. T. Houghton. This room was heated by hot-water coils (like the Lavatory), in addition to the open fire - ventilated into an extract shaft, very modern and most

---

27    David Shorney

welcome with all that cigar smoke. This was definitely a male domain and they would have smoked, drank their whiskey and swopped *risque'* anecdotes here without fear of offending the ladies. There was a wonderful collection of South American curiosities including clay *Inca idols* and a *mummy* of an Indian chief, dessicated by the dry air and burning sand of the desert rather than by being embalmed. The 'Celebrity at Home' article of 1888 mentions *'clay figures and 'whistling jars' from the graves of the Incas.'* These artefacts would have given the Colonel ample opportunity for recounting his Chilean adventures for the edification of his male guests, and no doubt in the absence of ladies, there were no holds-barred.

Caricaturists at the time loved to portray the Colonel smoking a fat cigar, but by his own admission, he never actually smoked! So the cigar-makers of the time who advertised their wares *'as smoked by Colonel North The Nitrate King',* would by today's standards be contravening trades description (non-existent at the time of course). This room was used by the college before the Second World War, as one of its main lecture rooms. That is quite a change of use - pleasure dome to font of knowledge.

## Morning Room

This room was essentially a ladies sitting-room, where the ladies spent the early part of a day and would usually be a room that got the sun in the morning. However, unlike the Boudoir, males were not entirely excluded.

## Lounge

Few descriptions of this room exist, although Wilkinson's auction catalogue lists it as a *Conservatory Lounge* – it was located across the bottom of the Eastern Corridor. Hampton's catalogue mentions that this room is *'heated by hot water in long ornamental iron casings with marble tops'*– there certainly were a variety of heating methods utilised in the Mansion, evidence of the Colonels engineering background and penchant for modernity. Shorney has a photograph on Page 26 of *Teachers in Training* which shows the lounge at the far end of the Eastern wing and another on Page 65 showing a *student's lounge*. In its day as a college this room seems to have been the student's Common Room where they could relax, chat and knit or do needlework.

**The Lavatory**

This *smallest of rooms* would not generally (and most definitely not in polite Victorian society) be one which would be expected to draw gasps of admiration and I am sure most do not get a passing mention,

Image 24; Lavatory - Then & Now

even those in the grandest of grand houses. However, the Colonel's *'Gentlemen's WC'*, facing the Billiard Room elicited the praises of even the sacked architect Cutler, who had to admit that it was indeed a *'wonder to behold'* and the whole effect *'refined , and pleasing'*. Even Jill Franklin in *'The Gentleman's Country House and its Plan 1835-1914'*, while disappointingly omitting a complete section on Avery Hill Mansion, does include Cutler's illustration of the Lavatory from the original plans. Franklin comments on the absence of plumbed-in washbasins from country houses at the time but notes that *'provision at Avery Hill was outstandingly lavish'*. I had wondered why the *fixed wash-basins* had elicited a mention as an innovation at the time, and Franklin explains that plumbed-in wash-basins were considered insanitary, with the Victorians being obsessed with noxious air lingering within the pipework.

The marble mosaic flooring was by the company of Burke & Co (this is from Edmundson), so not the same people who did the rest of the mosaic flooring, who we are told were Italian workmen. The stained-glass windows were designed and manufactured by Campbell Smith & Co. (also responsible for the *'sepia cartoons'* of the staircase window panels), well known church window makers of the time who remain in business to this day. This room made architectural history with its aforementioned set of fixed marble-topped washbasins and the striking tiled *chifonnier* – this is the sideboard with the plate-glass mirror, arched galleries and pierced brass-work beneath. Heating coils were placed within the faience enclosure under the large plate-glass mirror, very innovative, but we don't know how well they worked. The tiled *chifonnier* and marble-topped wash-basins are surviving testament to the splendour and opulence of the house. Basin fittings are aluminium and not plated with the centre basin originally fitted with shower douche, and spray attachment for *'shampooing'* (Victorian gentlemen seem to have never missed an opportunity for grooming), fine examples of the work of George Jennings of Lambeth. Raffles Davison suggests *'there are few examples of faience work in the country, so excellent in their* way, both as to material and colour, as the lavatory and one small enclosed court with garden and fountain (Garden Court)'. In his opinion 'from an architectural point of view, these are amongst the sights of the house'. The ladies don't seem to have been accommodated with such luxury!

This magnificent room is the sole survivor of the demolition of the eastern wing and that only by virtue of having been in use at the time, as part of the changing – rooms of the ladies college, otherwise it would most certainly have faced the wrecking-ball along with of the rest of the east wing in 1947.

## The Strong Room

'the strongest of strong rooms in the world', gushed the Yorkshire Post of May 1896. Victorians were very much given to superlatives:- every man with a few £100k was the richest man, every passable-looking society lady the most beautiful woman.

The Strong Room was reached by a flight of stairs next to the Lavatory - and where better to stash one's valuables than beneath the Lavatory!. As well as housing the Colonel's valuables, including his vast collection of ceremonial plate, both silver and gold, it also served as a repository for the jewellery of female overnight guests. The room measured 15 feet by 11 feet and was secured with heavy double iron doors. This room seems to have been constructed as a miniature fortress beneath the house, with floors many feet thick and walls of solid granite blocks, the whole with many secret burglar alarms – all very James Bond, and must have been a very unique talking point on the walks that the Colonel conducted for the amusement of his guests – and of course to show off. The British Architect of Sep 1889 gives construction costs of £2000 for this room alone.

David Shorney's plan of the Mansion in his 1990 booklet (an extract from 'Teachers in Training'), shows just the ground floor *unfortunately, although he briefly describes the first floor – furthermore, both Greenwich Archives and Avery Hill archive, have illegible copies of the first floor plan which seem to be enlarged copies of a small plan on one of Cutler's drawings. This is most disappointing as the Turkish Bath, which I would consider as being one of the most interesting features of the house, was on the First Floor.*

## White Marble Staircase (leading to first floor):-

The staircase itself being of white marble with a gilt and white ornamental wrought-iron balustrade with maple hand rail.

I do find it odd that the Colonel did not opt for a grand central staircase rising from the Entrance Hall, perhaps because it was just a two-storey building for most of its length. Franklin throws some light on this when she says that by mid-Victorian times, *staircases* were generally separated from the main hall as they would only have been used by the family and any guests staying, with the most splendid social occasions being confined to the ground floor – so most of the Colonel's visitors and those guests who were not staying overnight were confined to the ground floor.

### Staircase Window Panels

Raffles Davison mentions these, and research indicates they lit the stairwell of the white marble staircase. He remarks on the '*sepia cartoons*' designed and drawn by Mr. Smith of Campbell, Smith and Co., depicting *The Muses* and *The Elements*. He found these giving '*effects of delicacy*' but yet '*virile and characteristic*', unlike much of the current tastes which he found rather insipid, however, he found '*work like this adds much to the charm of an interior*'. The two images I have seen depicting *Air* and *Water* show two completely nude nymphs and these must have been the panels that the domestic staff found quite shocking, as stated in accounts held at Greenwich Archives, of people recalling

Image 25; Sepia Cartoons

stories told by relatives who had been in service at Avery Hill during the Colonel's time.

A photo from David Shorney's book (See Image 26a below) shows panels overlooking the stairwell but it is not clear if these show *The Elements*, however those further down the corridor may depict *The Muses*?

**First Floor Corridor**

Opening off this corridor were the sixteen principal bedrooms (27 bedrooms in total), all with dressing-rooms attached, marble wash-stands and *night commodes. One of the bedrooms (presumably principal), opened on to a large balcony with mosaic flooring.*

It had seemed unthinkable at first, that the Colonel, with his engineering background and love of the latest gadgetry, would have designed his bedrooms *without* bathrooms, given his magnificent lavatory and Turkish Bath. However, it is worth noting that even though it would have been possible, bathrooms were not considered essential or even desirable at this time, given the Victorian obsession with 'catching a chill' and the fear that plumbing harboured all sorts of potentially lethal *miasma*. Bathrooms were seen as a positive health hazard even as late as the 1920's, with Lady Fry, sister-in-law of the renowned architect Alfred Waterhouse, declaring '*bathrooms were only for servants*'. That is not to say that the Victorians went unwashed, as free-standing baths would be placed in front of the fire in either bedroom or dressing-room and laboriously filled by servants with jugs of hot water from the kitchen. Franklin adds however, that after 1840, new houses would hardly ever be without one bathroom for the exclusive use of the master and mistress. A well-trained pair of maids could *do* a bedroom in ten minutes – this included bed-dressing, emptying slops and replenishing the fire.

After checking Wilkinson's catalogue for the 1896 auction, it lists two other bath rooms and two closets (WC's?) on the First Floor.

Image 26a; First Floor Corridor

Image 26b; First Floor Corridor

Image26b below of the *First Floor Corridor,* must show some of the *9 Japanese Panels* as listed in Wilkinson's Contents Sale Catalogue of 1896. In 1880, Cutler the architect, had published a book on Japanese art – there was a vogue at this time for all things Japanese – It is therefore understandable that Cutler would have worked Japanese-inspired designs into his plans for the Mansion.

The corridor walls were hung with rich crimson silk velvet and *Gobelins* tapestry (Wilkinson catalogue says 6 on corridor and 2 on the spacious landing- this doesn't tie up with the 9 in Contents Catalogue) with lighted and stained glass windows (catalogue states 14 on corridor and 4 on the landing), some representing the *Muses* and *Elements*. The stained-glass windows were on the corridor to the left overlooking the service buildings to the front of the house, not the best of views, hence the obscuring windows, whereas those bedrooms on the other side of the house overlooked the garden.

Also opening off this corridor was the magnificent three-roomed **Turkish Bath**:-

Turkish Baths were extremely popular in Victorian times and seen as beneficial for the treatment of many conditions including; rheumatism, arthritis, and sciatica, by improving circulation, flushing out toxins and

Image 27; Turkish Bath

offering a general toning effect on the body. However, it is unlikely that North included an extremely grand one in his house purely for medicinal purposes, it was probably more like pure extravagance and for the indulgence of his male guests. It is odd that in her book, Jill Franklin gives no examples of Turkish Baths when they were such a popular extravagance, featuring in many of the grand Victorian country houses.

Accessed via a small lobby with double doors, the three-roomed Turkish Bath of Gothic design, was also accessible from Colonel North's bedroom, so his must have been the last on that corridor. The temperature would increase as one progressed from room to room. There must have been niches in the walls as we are told the walls were *'lined with statuary'*. The first of these rooms, the frigidarium or cool room, where one started and finished one's Turkish Bath experience, was lined in red and white marble with a large wardrobe, WC, washbasins and a spray bath. Here, the bather would spray himself (and he surely would be a he rather than a she) with cold water before proceeding to the next room. This was the tepidarium or warm room which was lined with grey and white marble as was the final and hottest room, the calidarium, which was furnished with marble benches for relaxation. Surmounting the whole structure which measured 35ft square, an octagonal roof with arches lined in Burmantofts faience in white and two shades of red.

As Shorney says *'Avery Hill was a house built for the twentieth century, it was built to bemuse, dazzle and impress and could justly claim to be among the foremost of the palaces of the Victorian nouveaux-riches in the last decade of the nineteenth century'*.

And nowhere is this more evident than in contemporary descriptions of this magnificent feature.

Surprisingly, Edmundson devotes just a couple of pages to the description of the house, making just a passing mention of *'an ornate Turkish Bath'*, which in reality was a this stupenduously decorated 3 room extravanganza, which, had it survived, would surely have been the best Victorian example of such a structure in the United Kingdom. The rare accounts of the Bath, mention that the supporting arches were lined in *Burmantofts faience* without giving an explanation as to what exactly this was and having now discovered that this was an architectural ceramic finish (glazed terracotta) perfected by the Leeds company of Burmantofts; it is entirely fitting that a proud son of Leeds like the Colonel, should be a patron of the workmen and materials of his Yorkshire home town.

Taken from Malcolm Shifrin's blog www.victorianurkishbath.org:-

> *'Among those impressed by the design and furnishing of the bath was the author of the detailed account which appeared in The Builder.*
>
> *The entrance was through a lobby—a very short passage with a door at either end—to help retain the heat within the Turkish bath area. This led into the largest room of the three, more a lavatorium than a frigidarium. To the right of the entrance was a toilet and a large walk-in cupboard for towels and, if necessary, bathers' clothes, and on the opposite wall was a bath and washbasin. Opposite the lobby was the door leading in to the marble-floored tepidarium. Although this was square in shape, the ceiling was octagonal, supported by arcading. On the right, a horseshoe arched window over-looked a courtyard (this must relate to the Garden Court) and white marble benches lined two of the walls. On the left was the arched opening to the calidarium.*
>
> *This was rectangular and had an arched window opposite the entrance. Below this was a lattice-covered compartment through which hot air entered the bath. The windows in both hot rooms consisted of two panes of glass with a heat insulation gap between them. The other two walls had white marble benches, partly positioned within high arched niches*
>
> *With its tiled walls, marble floors, and door fittings of silver plate, North's private Turkish bath was surely unique and, before it was*

*destroyed during a Second World War bombing raid, outshone either of the two extant private baths, Wightwick and Cragside.'*

Shifrin is wrong in his conclusion that the Turkish Bath was destroyed during a bombing raid, as the reality was far more tragic, it being demolished by the council in 1947 along with the rest of the Eastern wing, due to years of neglect of the fabric of the house during the war years and afterwards, with the result that it was deemed to be beyond repair.

I did ask Will Robley of UOG ,what the Turkish Bath was used for during the early days of the college prior to demolition in 1947. He said they held *weaving* classes there. We agreed it must have been chilly surroundings with all that ceramic. We also questioned the vandalism of destroying such a unique structure. Early student Mary Kay (1918-19) remembers '*occasionally bagging a bath in the 'forbidden bathroom'*. Is she talking about the Turkish Bath? She also mentions how those students who were lucky enough to live in the main building, loved its beauty and surroundings.

Also at the back on the First Floor were various service rooms; a housemaid's room, Box Room, Work Room with two bedroom above, Nursery and two bedrooms another bath room and WC.

Approached by a separate staircase from the Back Hall (is this Cutlers Visitor's Staircase?) three Men's Bedroom's – these would be the *Bachelor quarters* which at this time were always incorporated into large houses in order to segregate the young men from both the unmarried ladies of the house and female guests and the female staff. Victorian men couldn't be trusted to keep their impulses under control!!

**Second Floor** (*attic floor*)

Another four bedrooms and various storage rooms with a staircase leading to:-

## The Tower

This is the tall square structure visible on all contemporary postcards. With flag-mast and arched open viewing areas, it gave commanding views of the surrounding countryside, according to some of the early female trainee teachers (during the Mansion's time as a teachers training college), who were lucky enough to have access to it.

## Engine House and Chimney Tower

North the engineer is nowhere more evident than in his state-of-the-art heating and ventilation systems for his new house. Centrally-heated by circulation of hot water delivering warm-air via hidden coils. Very modern!

Electricity for the Mansion was generated in a separate three-roomed boiler-house which is that very large building to the west of the main house with the huge chimney the size that one normally only sees on Victorian hospitals. Raffles Davison informs us that the installation was to cope with 750 incandescent lamps and arc-lights for the Winter Garden. The *Electric Light House,* we are told, contains *Engine Room, Boiler House* and *Accumulator Room* (battery storage), workshops and coal stores and all of this being under the superintendence of a Mr. Massey who was the Prince of Wales' own electrician. Buckingham Palace was only *electrified* in the mid to late 1880's and when The Savoy Hotel opened in 1889, the fact that it was *electrified* was a unique selling point. Indeed, when the Colonel's refurbished house was completed in 1890, very few public buildings were using electricity, let alone private dwellings. Mears in his *Cook Family Memoir,* recalls Cook's daughter Christian relating how her father was called out '*at all hours of the day and night*' by the Colonel. One weekend he was summoned to organise outside lighting for a last-minute outdoor event at one of the Colonel's parties. Another call in the middle of the night turned out to be something as simple as '*changing a light bulb*', but of course at this time domestic electricity was in its infancy and even minor problems would require expert attention.

Coincidentally, while taking a coffee break during my research, in the Uni's Café, I struck up a conversation with a *mature* student doing a PhD, his background was engineering and he was able to explain that an *accumulator* was an old name for a battery and yet he was *completely* ignorant of the history of the house and its fellow-engineer creator, John Thomas North – a deficiency that I hope I have encouraged him to rectify.

## The Stables

T. Raffles Davison in his Rambling Sketches No 710 opines:- '*It is a question if there are any finer stables to be found. They are 22ft deep and 15ft high, lined with teak dado and brown and grey majolica bricks above.....every stall and loose box ventilated and heated with hot water and steam, and lit by the electric light*'.

The stable were in a separate block beyond the Engine House and this structure is still standing today, though in altered form as they are now mostly obscured by an ugly 1970's UOG building. Here the Colonels horses were very comfortably housed as Raffles-Davison had observed, with ten stalls, six loose boxes and a horse bath. The coach-house could accommodate twelve carriages and there were additional store and harness rooms.

The 1891 census shows the stable accommodation housing the coachman and his wife and their two grow-up sons, mother-in-law and two boarders, all of whom were grooms. The stable block was utilised as laboratories with some classrooms in its time as a training college. Maybe it was thought prudent that the young ladies conducted their scientific experiments at some distance from the main building! Another wing was added in 1907 for a science block and this was so skillfully blended in with the existing structure that only the most discerning eye could detect the join. It does seem that additions/alterations made during the tenure of the ladies college were generally sympathetic to the original house and constructed in the same style and red brick. Alas, the same could not be said of more recent additional wings as a complete hotch-potch of styles and materials has been the result.

## Stud Farm and Stables

It was by sheer chance on one of my visits to Avery Hill, that a sign in the public car park pointing to *Stud Groom Cottage* alerted me to the existence of the Stud Farm and Stables, all still standing although boarded-up. Set some distance away from the main house, beyond the current public car park, and still fairly intact, if woefully neglected, many visitors are still ignorant of its existence. Wilkinson's auction catalogue lists Stud Groom's house with six rooms, twenty-two timber-built loose-boxes and twelve brick-built and tiled loose boxes, and a harness room. It is obvious from the size of this complex, that the Colonel was serious in his pursuit of raising Derby winners, the stud contained 40-50 racehorses (according to *The King of Avery Hill*). Due to the size of the operation, it is easy to appreciate how much money the Colonel must have spent on his passion for race-horses and why he was advised to divest himself of his bloodstock in 1894.

Wilkinson's auction catalogue also mentions;-

> *'Five Vineries, Peach House and Fig House and many other greenhouses cultivating various other fruits and vegetables*
>
> *Extensive Pleasure Gardens – Laid out in Terraces with Tennis and Croquet Lawns*
>
> *Rosary (Rose Garden) Kitchen Garden and Orchard'*

Wilkinson's auction catalogue of 1896 lists the property being sold with 143 acres, whereas by the time of the Hampton's sale in 1901, it was with 84 acres.

# Chapter Eleven

## Sporting pastimes of the two and four-legged variety

The Colonel was a real lover of sports of all kinds and a popular member of what Guy Deghy in his 1958 memoir '*Paradise in the Strand*', calls the *Manly Cult*, predominantly composed of men of the *turfing* fraternity. He seems to have been happiest when surrounded with like-minded sporting individuals discussing their latest wins and acquisitions, whether of the canine or equine kind.

R.R.C. Gregory in '*The Story of Royal Eltham*', remembering North says ;-

'*The turf had no more generous and sportsmanlike patron. His horses ran straight. He trained and raced them because he had the true Yorkshire man's instinct for sport.*'

Gregory goes on to say;-

'*His keen interest in the welfare of national sport is illustrated by the fact that he was one of the originators of the national testimonial to W. G. Grace, the veteran cricketer. On the dedication page of W.G.'s book 'A Hundred Centuries' we find the following 'To Colonel John Thomas North, a thorough all-round sportsman and the first subscriber to my national testimonial fund. I dedicate this book (Signed) W. G. Grace July 1895'.*

Apparently there had been three crofts on the Avery Hill estate, in one of which Grace had lived - I think I got this information from Hunting's dissertation for the Faculty of Architecture at Woolwich Polytechnic 1999 'Avery Hill and it's Winter Garden' held at Greenwich Archives G7200 – although Will Robley of UOG was unaware of this. These crofts were demolished due to the main Bexley Road being re-directed during the Colonel's building works.

Although a keen all-round sportsman, North's particular interest was in racehorses and greyhounds, both of which he kept in some style at Avery Hill. The refurbishment of the Mansion had included a centrally-heated stable block where around sixty horses were kept in training. Russell claims that the Colonel's racing colours were copied from the Chilean flag which was blue and white, with a white star, the star being also worked into the Colonel's newly-acquired coat of arms. Bennion Booth in '*Palmy Days*', describes the racing colours as:- '*light blue, with primrose five-pointed stars, primrose sleeves, scarlet cap*'.[28] However, a volunteer at Holy Trinity in Southend Crescent, the North's local church, assures me that the Colonel's racing colours were black and white, and he gave the local scout group the 2nd Eltham, permission to incorporate his colours in their uniform. So attentive an owner was North, that he had even installed a steam-room where animals who may have caught a chill, could *sweat it out* – the stables also seem to have been lined with tiles, the equine equivalent of the famous Turkish Baths!

It is co-incidental that Thomas Blenkiron, son of William the world famous (from 18th through 19thc) Eltham's Middle Park stud owner, and Colonel North, have their final resting place, almost side-by-side in St. John's Churchyard in Eltham. Apparently it was this same Blenkiron, who had first advised North to get into the livestock market.

---

28    Palmy Days – Edwardian Memories: Theatrical Sporting Gastronomic J.B. Booth Richards Press 1957

William Blenkiron was another Yorkshireman who had also made his *pile* in trade but whose real interest was in the breeding of thoroughbred horses, which he did with much success – the Middle Park Stud was the largest and most successful of its kind in the world and produced four Derby winners. The Colonel would have hoped to emulate the success of his neighbour. In 1866 William Blenkiron had endowed the *Middle Park Stakes* race at Newmarket, which has run annually since, much like the golf competition for the *North Scratch Medal* at Royal Blackheath Golf Club. Sadly, as with North, Blenkiron and his famous *stud* will be unknown to most Elthamites today, and no commemorative benches honouring either of these gentlemen, among the many recently (2017) installed in Eltham High Street.

The large complex of buildings comprising the stud are still standing just beyond the public car-park if one follows the sign indicating *Stud Farm Cottage*.

North's horses ran in most of the top race meetings, with the Colonel's name popping up regularly in all the *sporting* periodicals of the day. So keen was he that he even went as far as organising impromptu race meetings for the amusement of house-guests at Avery Hill, by running both guests and horses to Newmarket by special train – this was much to the consternation of the Colonel's trainers, as horses would be raced whether they had been pronounced fit or unfit. According to Booth, *Simonian* and *Nunthorpe* were the most successful of the Colonel's stud, with the latter carrying off both the *City and Suburban* and *Jubilee Stakes* of 1891.

North delighted in *tipping* his horses to friends and acquaintances, which is all very well as long as they are winning. The Leeds Mercury printed a story of the Colonel attending a performance at Leeds Grand Theatre, the evening before his horse *St. Simon of the Rock* was due to compete in the St. Leger race. A large crowd had gathered to witness the Colonel's arrival (he was always guaranteed to draw a large crowd as a celebrated son of Leeds) and loud cheers went up when they spotted the Colonel who seemed delighted with this reception. Facing the throng he shouted at the top of his voice '*Back St. Simon for a shop, boys*'. In the event, the colt took third place.[29]

Booth mentions that having had early success on the *turf*, with winnings of £20,000 in 1891, these then fell to £15,000 in 1892 and dwindled to just £9,000 in 1893. Guy Deghy in '*Paradise in the Strand: The Story of Romano's*', speaks of the misconception that *men of the turf* were as stupid as their extravagant bets might suggest and quotes Dick Dunn, uncrowned *king of the bookmakers:-*

> '*There's many a bloke I would lay to on the course that I wouldn't buy stocks and shares from*'

It seems Deghy himself may have had the Colonel in mind when he adds:-

> '*Therein lies a deep truth. Betting men are, more often than not, geniuses in the financial field, tycoons of industries, giants in every branch of commerce, brilliant scientists and clear-thinking men of action. But let them get near a bookmaker, and they become capricious children. Let them buy a horse, and while it is running they will behave like idiots. These things are, of course, highly misleading. Get them away from the horses, and you will find the shrewdest lot of business magnates, that can see through your best-laid plans and be two jumps ahead of you, with a beautiful checkmate to follow*[30]

Bennion-Booth in '*Palmy Days*', confirms that the Colonel was notoriously careless with his money outside of business, and especially so on the racecourse, where he had a habit of losing track of his bets. Booth also suggests that North did not have the best advisers and that those nominated to manage his horses were continually at loggerheads with his trainers.

---

29    Guy Deghy 'Paradise in the Strand The Story of Romano's' Pg 175 The Richards Press 1958
30    Taken from Edmundson's The Nitrate King

There are several newspaper accounts of poachers being active on the Avery Hill estate, some indeed being current and former employees of the Colonel. While he was a very generous man if he perceived genuine need, the Colonel was what would be termed a *vexatious litigant* if he thought he was being swindled, even if it was of a few *'grapes and apples'*, as an account in the Woolwich Gazette of 2nd Sep 1887 shows. This article describes Augustus Riddlewick, aged 56 of *2, Southwood Cottages*, appearing at Woolwich court accused of stealing grapes and apples from the Avery Hill estate. The accused had recently been dismissed from the Colonel's employ and one of the estate gardeners, when called as a witness, claimed to have seen the accused *'trying the peaches also'* in the hot-house, having come in through the billiard-room of the main house. Some other articles of the Colonel's property had recently been reported missing also, and when the accused was found to be in possession of two keys, one fitting the Colonels billiard-room and the other his hen house, the evidence seemed damning. Riddlewick's house was searched and several items belonging to the Colonel were found, including five silver spoons, some lamps and a money-box. The article does not state the punishment meted out but we can be sure it would have been quite severe.

In November 1888, North paid 850 guineas for a greyhound pup named *Fullerton*, a record price at the time for a dog that had only raced once. There is an interesting tale concerning the Colonel and a greyhound recounted by Guy Deghy in his *'Paradise in the Strand'* memoir of the *goings-on* amongst the habitués of the famous *Romano's* restaurant of that thoroughfare, of which it seems the Colonel was a regular:-

> *'It was Hugo Astley who once bought a greyhound in Romano's and within ten minutes sold it at a reasonable profit. Running into Col. North later that night, he was informed that the animal was worth probably ten times as much as Astley had got for it. That immediately set him scouring the bar for the man who had bought the dog, and from him he found out that he had already*

*resold it. Just before closing time, Hugo Astley tracked down the current owner of his former property; he was the fifth who had bought it in Romano's that night, and the price he wanted for it was higher than that suggested by Col. North.'*

This is most probably just one of those '*tall tales*' that the racing fraternity, who made up the bulk of Romano's customers, delighted in entertaining each other with. However, we can imagine the Colonel would be both flattered and amused in reading this. With *Fullerton* and his kennel-mate *Troughend* sharing first place at the Waterloo Cup in 1889, the Colonel would have felt his hunch in paying top-price for a relatively untried dog was well rewarded. Fullerton went on to win the Cup outright in the succeeding three years.

Image 28; Left to Right:- Harry, Colonel North, his trainer Dent holding Fullerton, brother Gamble second from right and other sporting types

161

Sadly the silver Waterloo Cups for 1889 (183 ounces), 1890 (156 ounces) and 1892 (a massive 544 ounces and 3ft tall) are amongst many other silver sports trophies listed in the Wilkinson Catalogue of 1898.

Bearing this in mind, I am inclined to think the following piece appearing as it did on 1st April was most certainly an *April Fools* piece:-

> *'Colonel North's famous greyhound Fullerton, the hero of four Waterloo Cups, has disappeared from his owner's place, Avery Hill, Eltham, Kent. Seems that after being defeated at Altcar last month, Fullerton was taken to Eltham, where he had been allowed to roam at will about the mansion and grounds. Friday last he was missed, and, notwithstanding diligent search in every direction, his whereabouts cannot be discovered. On Monday night it was reported that a dog answering Fullerton's description had been received at the Battersea Dogs' Home*[31]

Such was the dog's prestige, that when he died in 1899, having outlived his master by three years, his body was given for preservation and can today be seen at the Walter Rothschild Museum, now part of the Natural History Museum at Tring in Hertfordshire. An Eltham Society article entitled '*A Fabulous Eltham Dog-Collar*', which appeared in the May 1994 magazine, details a silver collar which had been presented to *Fullerton* for his winning performance at the Waterloo Cup at Altcar on 25th Feb 1892. This item had turned up at Sudbury auctioneers, *Oliver's*, in November 1993. The catalogue states the makers were Frederick Edwards and Edward Johnson, London 1891, the collar weighed 15 ¼ ounces and measure 6 inches in diameter. The auctioneers put an estimate of £150-180 on it, but on the day it went for a whopping £3,900! It was engraved:-

> '*Fullerton .....the property of Col. J.T.North trained by Edward Dent Winner of the Waterloo Cup 1889, 1890, 1891, 1892*'.

It was perhaps, inevitable, that North would be advised to reassess his sporting ventures, which despite the pleasure they gave him, must

31    Worcestershire Chronicle 1st April 1893

have become a severe drain on his purse, so much so that, in 1894 he was persuaded to sell both horses (including his stud) and dogs. A man called Tattersall was engaged to auction the horses and Tattersalls are to this day, the leading dealers in the bloodstock market. Despite a large turnout, many suggested that it was the Colonel's reputation for hospitality, which had attracted the usual free-loaders, enticed by the prospect of a good 'spread', while unlikely to be serious *buyers*. Disappointingly, buyers on the day were not prepared to pay the prices North had put on his animals – he had put reserves of 2-3000 guineas on many of his prize mares and the result was only twenty of the seventy lots sold at a total of just 3000 guineas. It was suggested that perhaps the Colonel had deliberately set the reserves unrealistically high being not entirely happy about letting go this most loved part of his life anyway.

This sale was widely reported:-

> *'One hears that Colonel North will shortly retire from the turf.*
> *The Nitrate King does not believe in playing a succession of losing*
> *games, his horses having been unfortunate for some time. It is*
> *playfully suggested that Colonel North is "going to the dogs," he*
> *means to maintain his hounds to bring him the fame and fortune*
> *which apparently are not forthcoming from his stables*[32]

On the contrary, the Colonel did intend to sell his greyhounds and this sale proved more successful and indeed, as the newspapers stated, the Colonel had been more successful in his pursuit of the sport of greyhound *coursing*. This pastime was very popular in Victorian times and drew huge crowds to top events such as the Waterloo Cup held at Altcar near Liverpool. Coursing involved two greyhounds chasing a live hare and is banned today in the United Kingdom, with greyhound racing itself, just about surviving while many greyhound tracks have closed down in the past 20 years, with the last London track at Wimbledon, closing in 2017. The kennels at Avery Hill were every bit as sumptuously appointed as the stables and the Colonels dogs would have been just as well looked after as his horses. Indeed, *The Dartford Express* of 18th Jan 1890 quoted

---

32   *Dundee Courier* 28th Nov 1892

a rather critical piece from *The Star* which described the sumptuous kennels at Avery Hill, with the dogs being fed on prime cuts of beef, while observing that the Colonel's labourers were paid just 18 shillings (less than £1) a week – those with families to keep, not being paid any more. In the circumstances, one can understand that an employee, with possibly a large family to feed, and seeing how the animals at Avery Hill ate better and lived more comfortably than himself, might be tempted to filch from the master. North's will must not have been amended after the sale of his dogs/horses as the probate of his will granted 6th July 1896 mentions authorising the trustees '*to keep up, with a view to beneficial realisation, his racing and breeding establishment establishments (including his greyhounds as well as his horses)*'.

North had a liking for most sports and a newspaper article '*Celebrity at Home,*' gives us insights into the Colonels many sporting pastimes. We are told that weekend guests at Avery Hill would be invited on shooting parties to nearby '*Oxley, Blackboy and Upper Rennets Wood*'. The Colonel also enjoyed stag-hunting at Farningham, indeed he was Master of the Mid-Kent Staghounds – at these meets, a stag would be brought in especially for the hunt as they are not native to this part of Kent. The Dartford Express of 9th Nov 1889 had an account of one such occasion which started and finished at *The Lion Hotel* (still standing and still a lovely inn). Much champagne was provided (and this was at breakfast – one might ask 'Would they be in a fit state to hunt?'). A stag was then released at about 1 o'clock and made off in the direction of Kemsing, we are told. The proprietor of *The Lion,* a Mr. Dunn, must have looked forward to the Colonel's visits, given his notoriously deep pockets and the great numbers of hangers-on with their unquenchable thirst, who were sure to form part of any jaunt.

North also joined the local Eltham Golf Club in 1892 (now the Royal Blackheath Golf Club) along with his son Harry. The '*North Scratch Medal*' was inaugurated in 1892 with a donated prize of £10 and continues to this day – the medal can be seen in the club museum, although this is not the original medal as this was replaced by the current gold Jubilee Medal of Queen Victoria , presumably by North's son Harry. During the *'Be a Local Tourist Eltham 25th March 2018'*, I joined the tour of Eltham Lodge, the club-house of Blackheath Golf Club, hoping to see the *North Scratch Medal* but the first thing the guide told us was that the museum was closed. On contacting the club, Secretary, Mark Hickson was good enough to give me a private viewing of the medal. Harry North was also Captain at the Eltham Warren Golf Club in 1920 – this was just across the Bexley Road from his home at Lemonwell. That year Harry died at the tragically young age of 53.

Colonel North also seems to have had an interest in football as he sent a banknote to an injured *West Bromwich Albion* player, who returned to the field with his head bandaged, during the 1896 Cup Final played at Crystal Palace.[33]

There was also cricket of course, with the *'Celebrity at Home'* article stating:-

> *John North like a true Yorkshireman, is as fond of cricket, running and healthy exercise as when he and 'Jack' Whitley (Director of the Italian Exhibition) sat on the same form at the school they went to in Leeds, before he was apprenticed to a millwright or dreamed of the existence of NaNo3*

The Colonel certainly did play cricket at Avery Hill and was even remembered by W.G.Grace in his 1895 *'History of a Hundred Centuries'* with its dedication to the Colonel (described in Gregory's History of Royal Eltham). The Colonel would also eagerly challenge members of the Tower Hamlets Volunteers when they were camped at Avery Hill, to sixty-yard sprints, so confident was he that he would even give his opponents a five-yard start. In later years friends would recall how the Colonel turned blue in the face following these exertions and was seriously warned against any more – an early manifestation of a heart problem, perhaps.

---

33    Friends of Avery Hill Park

# Chapter Twelve

## Kirkstall Abbey, Politics and other philanthropic gestures

I n addition to the many small acts of generosity, the Colonel undertook several charitable endeavors for which he has not been given sufficient credit, in my opinion. One of the largest of these was the purchase of Kirkstall Abbey and its subsequent bequest to the city of Leeds. The abbey stood on the estate of the Earl of Cardigan – the 7th Earl died leaving no heirs but lots of debt and so the Abbey and grounds went up for auction in December 1888 but failed to reach the reserve. Meanwhile, North met with two representatives of the Leeds Mechanics Institute at the Hotel Metropole (maybe staying here while works proceeded at Avery Hill). The Institute was in the process of opening a new boy's school and North in his capacity of '*famous son of Leeds*' as well as being a member of the Institute, would have been top of the list of people they would have wanted for the opening. North agreed to officiate and also contributed a generous £250 towards building costs. According to '*The Life and Career of the late Colonel North*', it was during this meeting that he heard of the plight of Kirkstall Abbey and decided he would buy it and present it to the city of Leeds. He recalled having fun in the grounds of the Abbey as a child, playing '*kiss-in-the-ring*'! His cheque dated 25th Nov 1889, in the sum of £10,000, survives and can be seen at the headquarters of Leeds local history group, The Thoresby

Society. Some accounts state that Kirkstall Abbey was bequeathed in the Colonels will but a Yorkshire Society plaque in the grounds states that Col. North purchased the Abbey and grounds in 1888 (he died in 1896) and gave them to the city – this plaque, unveiled in 1988 and subsequently moved to the Visitors Centre in October 2008 is all that remains to commemorate North's generous bequest.

Image 29; Kirkstall Abbey

In appreciation, the Leeds Borough Council made North an *honorary freeman of the borough* and this was presented to him in a silver casket which also held a small book containing a record of the Council resolution, with the names of all the Town Council and small watercolour views of the Town Hall and Kirkstall Abbey. This was another honorary title that must have given him a great sense of pride as he was always keen to acknowledge his humble Yorkshire roots, and let's be clear, North loved a *title*. At the ceremonial handing over of the cheque in Jan 1889, the Colonel started his speech, to loud cheers *'There is no doubt I have been prosperous even beyond my expectations, but what is the use of money if you don't spend it in the way it should be spent?'*. An additional £900 was donated by the Colonel for the purchase of more adjoining land *'for the children to play upon'*. After restoration the abbey was opened to the public in September 1895.

Kirkstall Abbey is only about a mile from the centre of Leeds and should be a *must* for any visitor to the city. None of the pictures I have seen get anywhere close to capturing the magnificence of this 12th century architectural marvel.

Another recipient of North's beneficience, was the *Leeds General Infirmary*, who received a £5,000 donation towards the building costs of a new wing. *The Engineering Department of the Yorkshire College* (forerunner of Leeds University) was another North beneficiary, receiving 2,500 guineas. There were also rumours that North intended to acquire the moor at Holbeck, the town of his birth, and present it to the city but there is no evidence to support this.

The Sidcup and District Times of 20th July 1888 describes the Colonel as a man of extremely generous disposition:-

> *'His happiest moments seem to be those when he is spending some portion of his wealth in giving pleasure to others....'* it goes on to mention *'the five or six hundred children from the Westminster backstreets who visited Avery Hill the other day, enjoyed a treat which will stick in the memories of most of them for many a year'*

David Shorney's notes in *Teachers in Training* add:-

> *'Travelling by train from Charing Cross to New Eltham station (Eltham at the time?), they marched behind their Vicar, Canon Furse, and their banners, from the station to Avery Hill, to*

*arrive in the park at 10:30 am to be entertained during the day with donkey rides, a Punch and Judy show and many other entertainments. Before returning to the station in the evening, each child received either a skipping rope or a necklace, or a set of battledore and shuttlecocks.* [34]

In similar vein, The Dartford Express of 1st Sep 1888 article *'Celebrity at Home'*, another *Hello* style profile of the Colonel:-

*'Success has not spoiled the natural modesty of John North and there is no brag and very little 'I' in his conversation'*

This article concludes rather poetically:-

*'Many monarchs and many princes have, in their day kept 'Royal Christmas' and given sumptuous feasts at Eltham, but possibly, after all, no regime was more universally popular than that which commenced when The Nitrate King moved his Court from the deserts of Tarapaća to the grassy slopes of Avery Hill'*

That same paper contained a more *tongue in cheek* account of the Colonel's charitable endeavors under *'Local Notes and Comments'* by *'Roamer'* of 31st Aug 1889:-

*'Charity is one of the easiest modes of obtaining a cheap advertisement. Many great men who have sprung from nothing, have found it pay wonderfully. Colonel North has just given a treat to the poor of Eltham. The feed was a very liberal one, and under each plate was a fully paid-up Nitrate Share!'*

The Yorkshire Evening Post of 29th June 1891, angry at the aspersions cast in court against the character of their fellow Yorkshireman during the case brought by his architect Cutler, defended their man robustly, claiming that he gave above £20,000 a year in charity without any fanfare.

---

34    D Shorney Teachers in Training Note no 12 on Chapter 1 pg 322

Now that he was an established *man of substance* and well-respected *pillar of the community*, North turned his attention to politics and as a precursor, applied for membership of the Conservative Carlton Club. This club had been founded in 1832, by Tory peers, MPs and gentlemen, as a place to coordinate party activity and it later played a major role in the transformation of the Tory party into its modern form as the Conservative Party. Lord Randolph Churchill (recipient of North hospitality at both the Hotel Metropole and Avery Hill) was one of his sponsors. There were hints that Churchill's sponsorship was not entirely without self-interest, his friendship with North having proved lucrative during the nitrate boom years. To smooth his way, the Colonel pledged £20,000 towards the club's election fund. Opportunity presented itself in the 1895 General Election, when North was chosen to contest the West Leeds seat against Herbert Gladstone, the incumbent Liberal MP for Leeds and youngest son of William Gladstone the Prime Minister, which, one imagines must have given him very much of a head-start over the good Colonel.

This is an extract from a letter that had been published many years earlier, in the Leeds Times of 28ᵗʰ Jan 1889 and was quite prescient in its observation:-

*'The cry has been started that the "Nitrate King" has been actuated all along by desire to represent his native borough in Parliament, and that the gift of Kirkstall Abbey and grounds, to his fellow-townsmen was nothing more nor less than a bid for popularity. Surely nothing could be more unworthy than such insinuations. I am not aware that the Colonel has any ambition for parliamentary honours—least of all, he has not caused such senseless rumours to be bandied about. Time enough to "look a gift horse in the mouth" when such a contingency arises, and when the inhabitants, both old and young, have experienced the pleasures of a holiday amid the hoary ruins of our grand old Abbey. In the meantime let us be charitable, and recognise the wisdom of the old adage, "Handsome is that handsome does".*

And it has to be said that the Colonel most definitely *did* handsomely, judging by his many charitable actions. However, even though North was immensely popular in his native Leeds, he would continue to prove a divisive figure, and was not always sure of being given an easy passage by the local press, especially the Leeds Mercury, who saw the Colonels philanthropies, purely as the oiling of political wheels – they urged their readers to ignore the Colonels siren call and re-elect Herbert Gladstone. Amongst the stories surrounding this event, it was claimed that North had all the white dogs in the city rounded-up and dipped in laundry blue (Conservative colour) and then let loose onto the streets of Leeds.

These are the last two verses of a popular music-hall tune of the time *'Where did you get that hat?'* – the references to North are not even that well *veiled*. A fellow-member of the Eltham Society, Margaret Taylor, had used this song to illustrate her 4th May 2008 walk entitled *'The Road to South America'*, wrote that this song had apparently been penned for the visit of Edward VII, who supposedly visited Avery Hill when Prince of Wales, although I have not seen any real evidence of such a visit:-

> *I once tried hard to be M.P. but failed to get elected*
> *Upon a tub I stood, round which a thousand folks collected*
> *And I had dodged the eggs and bricks (which was no easy task)*
> *When one man cried, "A question I the candidate would ask!"*
>
> **Chorus:-**
> *"Where did you get that hat? Where did you get that tile?.....*
> *(tile is 19th century slang for 'hat')*
> *When Colonel South, the millionaire, gave his last garden party*
> *I was amongst the guests who had a welcome true and hearty*
> *The Prince of Wales was also there, and my heart jumped with glee*
> *When I was told the Prince would like to have a word with me*

While North would have fancied himself as a public speaker, oratory was not one of his strong points, according to his critics; but if his speeches lacked *political substance*, they made up for this deficiency, in a delightfully down-to-earth bluntness which would have appealed to the ordinary folk of Leeds. In the few campaign speeches he did make, he promised government contracts for local industries and offered racing tips to the men. Amongst the ladies he distributed handkerchiefs bearing his portrait – one has to admire his panache! This was a great PR opportunity for a natural showman like John Thomas North, he was indeed in his element.

The Colonel was interviewed at the time in the Sketch, and jocularly claimed to have given Gladstone, who had after all, been in politics for fifteen years, a good run for his money considering his own brief two week campaign. He says he refused an invitation from the Prince of Wales himself to dine at Sandringham, due to his campaign commitments. He declares that, had there been women's suffrage, he '*would have beaten him into a cocked-hat*' as the women and children were all on his side!

On Election Day, there was free beer for all comers at the Conservative Club and a fleet of fire-engines ferrying voters to the polls. When, in time honoured tradition, the Colonel was presented with babies, he was likely to pat the children and kiss the mothers much to the amusement of onlookers. *I wonder what Mrs. North made of this?* At the count, the Colonel lost narrowly by 96 votes in a poll of 12,500, a remarkable achievement for a newcomer. The press were kinder to him in defeat, with the Leeds Mercury declaring '*Colonel North, while thoroughly at home as a sportsman, as a financier, and a tower of strength as a friend, was altogether impossible as a politician*'. Booth in '*Palmy Days*', mentions the Colonel having admitted that:- '*one of the bitterest disappointments of his life was his unsuccessful contesting of West Leeds against Herbert Gladstone in 1895 and he would have given anything to have won the seat*'. Booth asserts it was a pity as:- '*it is a reasonable certainty that he would have enlivened the House of Commons*'. And I have to agree with him.

The Colonel, never one to shy away from bold statements, also had something to say of the emerging *Temperance Movement,* that most

Victorian of *nanny-state* attempts to interfere in the private lives of those they deemed required saving from their own baser instincts. The Temperance Movement was a social movement which campaigned against the consumption of alcoholic beverages by highlighting the negative effects of alcohol on health and families. The Colonel had chaired a few meetings of *The Licensed Victuallers and Beersellers Association* at the *Lullingstone Castle* at Swanley Junction, where the subject of the increasing influence of the *Temperance Movement* arose. The Colonel declared that the Conservatives (his party) would never secure the temperance vote because they (the Temperance party) were fanatics. Waxing warm, the Colonel declared that:- '*if men could not come together, have a glass of something to drink and be hail fellows well met – why, they were not men at all!*'. This was greeted with much laughter and rapturous applause. The Victuallers could not have found a better ambassador than the Jolly Colonel.

# Chapter Thirteen

## Nitrate wanes ; Other Speculations

By the late 1880's the nitrate boom had already started to wane, primarily due to fluctuating demand from farmers due to reduced prices on their crops, plus the high tax imposed on nitrate exports by the Chilean government. The nitrate boom years of 1887-89 had run out of steam and overproduction and an overheated stock market prompted a crisis in the industry. However, by this time, North had already diversified into Australian gold and silver mines, trams in Egypt, industries in Belgium and even the travel business, with a planned hotel and leisure complex in Ostend. Closer to home, he bought the *Lynvi and Tondu Company* in 1889 which had coal mines in South Wales. North had heard of this business opportunity through his neighbour at nearby Southwood House, John Joseph Smith, who had been appointed receiver when this company went into bankruptcy. The asset was acquired for £150,000, but sold on to North's Western Navigation Syndicate for the inflated sum of £350,000. This was another of North's business transactions that was seen as less than ethical and there was more legal action arising from it, although not directly involving North. Some shareholders felt that Smith's actions had constituted a *conflict of interest,* as he had acquired a financial interest, while acting as liquidator. However, North's philanthropic gestures are still in evidence in Wales to this day, with the *Colonel North Memorial Hall* in Maesteg, of which his son Harry, had laid the foundation stone. Another donation of £500, was used towards the construction of the North's *Miners Library and Institute.* In addition, North had provided land to be used for the establishment of new schools to accommodate up to 1,000 local children. Also still standing in Maesteg is North's *Navigation Company* building.

Meanwhile, investment in other ventures like the Anglo-Belgian India Rubber Company in 1892, would prove more controversial. This company was owned by Belgian King Leopold II, but run as a private enterprise. Some of the worst aspects of European imperialism were perpetrated in the Belgian Congo region, where taxes on rubber extracts, were levied on all inhabitants. North's family had divested themselves of any interests in the Congo following the Colonel's untimely death in 1896 and thus avoided the embarrassment of being implicated in the investigation conducted by the British Government in 1903 and its devastating reports of human rights abuses that resulted.

By 1894, North's speculative instincts saw him looking to Australian gold mines for fresh opportunities, acquiring the *Londonderry Gold Mine* in Coolgardie, Western Australia. Initial exploration of the mine had proved promising and North and his associates floated the acquisition through the usual joint-stock company route on the London Stock Exchange, with a capital of £700,000. Unfortunately for investors the early findings did not materialise into the expected gold yields and so, understandably North faced the usual criticism in the financial press, with the Economist of 6th April 1895 stating that:- '*this was an extraordinary start for a property from which, only a few months ago, it was stated that £600,000 worth of gold could be taken in a month or two*'. More litigation arose from North's dealings with the *Londonderry* mine and this would continue even after his death. 1894 had also seen the Colonel expand into silver mining in Tasmania and then more gold mining in New Zealand and South Africa. There were also interests in tramways in Egypt, cement works in Belgium and factories in France. Reporting on conditions at the Belgian cement works, The Illustrated Buffalo Express of Dec 27th 1892 in 'A Talk With One of The Richest Men in the World', gave a positive verdict on the Colonel's business methods when it reported that he had taken a failing enterprise and quickly turned it into a flourishing business employing thousands of workers, for whom he erected both houses and churches. 'He has never had a strike and his people all like him'.

Further litigation arose following the acquisition of a French brewery. It does seem that maybe North was doing what a lot of businessmen did in the late 20th century and lived to regret, by diversifying from their core businesses and expanding too rapidly.

A hotel and leisure complex in Ostend was also under consideration, with North having negotiated with King Leopold in late 1895, the purchase, for £300,000, of a mile and a half of coastline on which he intended developing an upmarket tourist resort that would even have a casino to rival that at Monte Carlo, with North poised to invest up to one million sterling in the project. In 'The Life and Career of the Late Colonel North: How He Made His Millions: As Told By Himself' in 1896, claims the Ostend enterprise:- 'would combine the attractions of Rosherville (a popular Victorian pleasure-garden near Gravesend), Monte Carlo and the Hanging Gardens of Babylon' - typical North hyperbole. This account also claims that much of the North fortune was diminished in the storm that overtook the majority of his ventures and although it was not widely credited, he had retained an immense interest in several of the nitrate companies, long after most prudent men would have quitted them. This does not sound like North the shrewd businessman but then we know that he could be sentimental, if the occasion suited. Sadly this account also reports:- 'His dinners, lunches, house-boat at Henley and picnics at Ascot and Goodwood were conducted in princely style but his guests only returned it with their (calling) cards'.

In 1895 the Nitrate Steamship Company Limited had been created by North and his associates, for the shipment of nitrate from Chile to North America and Europe. Their ships numbered; *The Colonel J. T North*, *The Avery Hill* and sadly, the poignantly named *Juanita North* (after wife Jane), was launched eight days after the Colonels death.

# Chapter Fourteen

## 'Passed'; Death of the Colonel

There was no indication in the weeks leading up to his death, that the Colonel was in anything but his usual, rude good health. He probably ate and drank too much and of late had become rather corpulent and maybe more ruddy in the face, but nothing to alarm. The morning of Tuesday 5th May 1896 was unremarkable except for the arrival in the morning's post, of a letter from an impecunious artist who had three pictures for sale – his letter asked for five pounds for the lot. He must have heard of the Colonel's being a sucker for a sob story (as well as wanting to fill his Picture Gallery) – and he was not wrong in his assessment, as having read the letter, North told his valet to take the pictures, adding:- ' *The fiver may do the poor fellow some good and it won't hurt me*'. Before leaving for his office, the Colonel also had a meeting with an engineer to discuss the installation of *phonographic* equipment in the house. The phonograph was the forerunner to the gramophone and in its early incarnations seems to have been used for voice recording much like a *dictaphone* before being used for the playing of music on recorded cylinders – it is impossible to deduce what use the Colonel had in mind for his new - fangled equipment, but the engineer in him, would as always, have been fascinated by any new *gadgetry*.

At the usual time of 10am, the Colonel had left Avery Hill for his office in Gracechurch St. in the City of London, accompanied by his son Harry. He seemed in his usual good spirits. At around 2.45 he had a *light luncheon* of a dozen oysters and a bottle of stout. At 3pm the Colonel proceeded to chair a meeting of the *Buena Ventura Nitrate Company*, with his son Harry and brother Gamble in attendance. As the meeting proceeded, the Colonel was seen to turn pale and emitting a feeble groan, called for brandy and slumped back in his chair. Harry rushed to his father's side but the Colonel had already lapsed into a state of unconsciousness, from which he would not recover – he was pronounced dead at around 3.50pm. At just 54 years of age, John Thomas North was no more.

Image 30; Colonel North & Harry

The shells from the oysters taken at lunch were sent for scientific analysis but nothing untoward was found and an inquest returned a verdict of '*death by natural causes*' with the Colonel's own Dr. Jeken[35], who had attended him for 13 years, declaring heart failure as the probable cause of death – some newspaper accounts of the time give apoplexy (stroke) and even dyspepsia, although death from indigestion seems a bit extreme. The '*Inquest on Colonel North*' as related in The Times on May 7th, quotes how Harry North recalled his father slumping forward shortly after having written the word '*Passed*' against a resolution on the agenda.

The Economist, ever a North detractor, concluded in tones of gross and ungracious snobbery in '*Millionaires in Business*' on 9th May 1896:-

> '*He was from first to last just a workman who had made a great fortune and who loved to proclaim it by extravagant expenditure, by ostentatious display, and by bearing everybody down.*'

Not surprising from a paper that was generally hostile to the new breed of '*self-made millionaires*' in commerce and viewed them as perhaps '*getting above their station*' in mingling with men '*far above them in birth and cultivation*'. However, their account does not reflect well on the upper echelons of society either, who it seems were quite happy to be entertained and given insider financial information relating to new stock flotations, while holding their noses at reciprocating the Colonel's kind hospitality.

Amongst the obituaries, I particularly like this from The Kentish Independent on the '*Death of Colonel North*', which appeared on the day of the funeral May 9th 1896:-

> '*He was one of the toilers of life, and he never desired or pretended to be anything else. Those, therefore, who sneer at his manners and speech, ought rather to give him credit for his honesty and consistency, and dwell rather upon the goodness of the man,*

---

35   R.R.C. Gregory in The Story of Royal Eltham 1909, states that Dr. Jeken had practised in Eltham for the greater part of the last half-century

*his generous genial qualities, and the example he offers by his industry, courage, and perseverance, and put to the credit the fact that he was not one of the social order to whom the good things of the world have come by no merit of the individual.'*

The Sketch of May 13<sup>th</sup> 1896 had the following:-

*'North's wide range of business interests saw him as chairman of no less than 11 companies and even then he was always on the lookout for new opportunities. He went to Chile to instruct the nitrate plants in the use of the newly-invented steam-plough. Sometimes a dogmatic and belligerent chairman when confronted with an angry crowd of shareholders, as at the meeting of the Londonderry Mine, where he threw a bundle of share certificates at the assembled, which landed on the head of a reporter who sent it flying back at the top table, narrowly missing the Colonel. This was just the sort of lively board-meeting that our hero seemed to take most pleasure in – however, the customary vote of thanks for the chairman was not always forthcoming. The Colonel's worst fault was perhaps, his perpetual optimism and yet with all his shortcomings, he was a man who made himself liked in most quarters and would be missed by even his most hostile critics.'*

The South American Journal's opinion was:-

*'Though not a man of much culture or high educational attainments, he was eminently gifted with the qualities of judgement, prevision and promptitude, which lead the way to conspicuous success in business enterprise or speculation.'*

On hearing of the Colonel's death, William Howard Russell, who had accompanied the Colonel on his final trip to Chile, wrote in his diary:-

*'It was not a surprise but it was a great shock to think that I shall never again see or suffer the great, kindly, blusterous Boreas (Greek*

*god of the North Wind and a play on the Colonel's name)), so full
of goodness. To me and my wife he was ever courteous considerate
and attentive...He was dearly loved and was in many ways
loveable.*[36]

Gregory in '*A History of Royal Eltham*', talks of the genuine outpouring
of grief displayed by the people of Eltham:- '*Every shop and public house
in the village was closed on the day of the funeral*', with the blinds of every
house in the High Street being lowered as a mark of respect. Some 800
wreaths were received and the funeral procession was so long that, '*when
the church was reached, the last carriage had not yet left the keepers cottage
in the Bexley Heath Road*'. The Belgian Ambassador attended the funeral
representing Leopold II, King of the Belgians, while the Khedive of
Egypt sent a message of condolence to Mrs. North.[37] Blakemore asserts
that the telegraph office in Eltham was so inundated with messages of
condolence to the North family, that it had to increase its staff and
remained open at night from May 6th-9th 1896 – he went on to say
that J.T. North deserved to be remembered in the country of his origin
as he was in that South American republic on the other side of the
world.

Again from Gregory:-

> '*the name of Colonel North will long be remembered by the
> parishioners of Eltham. His bountiful hospitality, his thoughtful
> consideration for poorer neighbours, especially at Christmas time,
> when it was his annual custom to provide every cottage with
> the good things needful for the season's festivity. His patronage
> of local sport and his readiness to give of his wealth towards the
> maintenance of local institutions, charitable and otherwise, are
> memories that will long be associated with his name and with
> Avery Hill*'.

---

36   John Black Adams 'The Life of Sir William Russell' 1911
37   RRC Gregory A History of Royal Eltham Pg 319

David Shorney in '*A Brief History of the Mansion at Avery Hill*' *1984* (revised 1990) writes that:-

> '*Colonel North has remained a legendary figure in South East London.*'

I beg to differ, it was because of the dearth of material relating to the Colonel and his Mansion, that I was prompted to embark on this account. I was also shocked to discover that North has not even been remembered with a commemorative *bench* in Eltham High Street, when even the most minor soap-opera and pop stars have been honoured in this way. Who will remember them in a hundred years? Hopefully, Avery Hill Mansion and Winter Garden will still be there and we will therefore continue to hear the name of Colonel North.

# Chapter Fifteen

## Robber Baron or Jolly Colonel?

The term "robber baron" began to be used in the early 1870's to describe a class of extremely wealthy businessmen who used ruthless and unethical business tactics to dominate vital industries. The term robber baron had originated in Germany to describe unscrupulous medieval lords who levied essentially illegal tolls on the primitive roads crossing their lands. The metaphor was then taken up in the late 1850's to describe the unethical and monopolistic business practices amongst the emerging American industrialists of the late 1850's – men such as Cornelius Vanderbilt and J.P. Morgan.

North was always what (in popular parlance) we would call a *Marmite* figure, he was either loved or hated, no in-betweens. Whilst many newspapers eulogised him as a self-made man who rose from humble beginnings through hard work and a propensity to take risks, his old nemesis, The Economist, saw no reason to let-up in its criticism of North, even in death, witness The Economist '*Millionaires in Business*' May 9th 1896 extract above. The Financial News was also critical while the Financial Times tended to be a defender.

The Colonel's home county were understandably defensive of the reputation of one of their most celebrated and generous son's with

'*The Yorkshire 'Owl'* column in a Leeds newspaper of 13th May 1896 opining:-

> '*Colonel North is dead. There is not a heart in the whole city that will not beat with sympathetic vibration at the sad news, and few indeed are the persons who will not consider his loss in the light of a personal affliction.*'

Indeed, with the Colonel's passing there were sure to be many dry mouths amongst that vast band of hangers-on and spongers that he always seemed to attract.

The writer went on to describe North as probably the greatest man Leeds had ever produced, who had been instrumental in drawing attention to Leeds, and while being '*no great genius*' and not having any of those gifts that might ensure their owner a niche in the temple of fame, what he did have was a *heart* and it was by his far-reaching and spontaneous generosity that he became known:- '*the spoilt child of Fortune very often, but never spoilt in those better and finer feelings that show the true hearted 'man'.*' Kirkstall Abbey would forever stand as a lasting and most beautiful monument to his unequalled generosity, this obituary ended by declaring North:- '*the prince of all good fellows*' - a compliment the Colonel would have been most proud of.

North was easily cast as the '*evil Robber Baron*', while ignoring his huge contribution to the development of the nitrate industry in Chile/Peru which became the main source of revenue for an otherwise poor country. North's business model has been likened to the Ponzi schemes of the 20th century, where profits were initially paid from capital derived from new entrants to the scheme, but if we are to use financial terminology, maybe *venture capitalist* is a fairer description of North as he identified opportunities, took risks and used capital to exploit such opportunities. In the export of British capital and enterprise in the nineteenth and early twentieth centuries, the key role was often played by individual entrepreneurs who created the necessary interest among the investing public in the potentiality of overseas resources and who made possible significant developments in the areas of their operations, largely by the force of personal example. Such a man was John Thomas North, the principal promoter of an industry and trade that was the economic prop of the Latin American state of Chile from the 1880's until the First World War. I believe John Thomas North deserves a permanent place in the history of Chile and in the history of British commercial relations with Latin America.

Although his life was not long when measured in years, within that comparatively small compass he managed to compress such a life of variety and adventure as would have been enough to fill the lives of a dozen ordinary men.

The philanthropies of two of North's American contemporaries, John D. Rockefeller and Andrew Carnegie, could not save them from being dubbed *robber barons* by later generations who were all too quick to judge and condemn these men posthumously, while being unwilling to acknowledge their contribution to civic society. Even Henry Tate, the *sugar baron,* whose name graces countless galleries and libraries to this day, funded from his bequests to the nation, has had his reputation put under the microscope, with claims that his fortune was based on slavery, which it was not. By all accounts, Tate was a kindly employer, as was North –I have already quoted from above from The Illustrated Buffalo Express of 1892 reporting on conditions at North's Belgian cement works which gave a positive verdict on the Colonel's business methods claiming that he had taken a failing enterprise and quickly turned it into a flourishing business employing thousands of workers, for whom he erected both houses and churches.

*'He has never had a strike and his people all like him'.*

If money was legally earned, it is not for the *morally outraged* to seek to deprive the multitude by tainting donations made in good faith.

Had North been more of a social crusader in the mould of his contemporaries - Cadbury, Rowntree and Lever, history may have been kinder to his memory – unlike them, North has not had recognition for the many philanthropic gestures made during his lifetime. With the prevailing trend for seeing history through the prism of current mores, subjects such as the North have not be seen as fitting subjects for further investigation. However, there is a new breed of historian who are looking to shine a light on those like North, abandoned by the history books due to the prevailing left-wing narrative of our time.

In contrast, R.R.C. Gregory the author of 'The Story of Royal Eltham' (1909), and a contemporary of North's wrote effusively:-

> 'He had a niche for himself in the popular imagination. The most rabid Socialists had a good word for 'the Colonel'. He was so thoroughly human in all he did that envy of his riches was lost in a sense of good fellowship with him. He spent his wealth in regal fashion, not only in the entertainment of his hosts of friends and acquaintances, but also in public purposes and in charity. A man of ideas, enterprise, and financial daring – thoroughly English in his frankness, breadth and variety of character – can ill be spared'.

Such was the prevailing perception in Eltham of the Colonel, amongst his contemporaries.

Perhaps a commemorative bench on Eltham High Street is the very least we owe to the memory of the good Colonel.

# Chapter Sixteen

## The Aftermath

The Colonels widow Jane, must have felt that the anxiety concerning his house rebuilding and numerous law suits, were probably contributing factors in her husband's untimely death and she lost no time in putting the Avery Hill estate up for sale – the Colonel had died on 5th May and the estate went up for sale on July 27th. The speed with which she did this would indicate that maybe she longed for a quieter, less ostentatious life. She seems to have been happy to leave behind the Mansion for the far more modest *Red Croft* which stood at the junction of Court Road and Court Yard in Eltham - This house was demolished in 1960 to make way for the building of Moat Court. Jane North died aged 81 on May 15th 1924 and is buried with her husband and many other family members in St. John's churchyard in Eltham:-

Jewell North (younger son) who had been killed in action in France 1918 aged 34

Harry North (elder son) died aged 53 in 1920 along with his wife Jessie who died aged 73 in 1942

Emma Lockett OBE (daughter) died Dec 1941 aged 73 and her husband George Alexander Lockett died aged 68 in 1923

**Concerning the Colonels Will:-**

The Lincolnshire Chronicle of 3rd July 1896 had this account:-

> *'The will of the late Colonel John Thomas North, of Avery-hill, Eltham, will be proved, it is expected, in the course of a few days, and estate duty, it is understood, will be paid on just about £500,000, as value of his estate.'*

South Wales Daily News 6th July 1896:-

> *'LATE COL. NORTH'S WILL. Probate of the will of Col. John Thomas North, of Avery-Hill, Eltham, who died on the 5th of May last, aged 54 years, leaving personal estate of the net value of £263,866, has now been granted. The will bears date January 25th, 1895, and he bequeaths in trust such sum as will produce £2,000 a year, and 30 per cent, to pay to the trustees of his estate during the continuance of this trust £500 a year each for 10 years, and 2250 a year each afterwards whilst the trust continues. The present trustees are his widow, Mrs Jane North his son, Mr Harry North his son-in-law, Mr George Alexander Lockett; and his solicitor, Mr John Wreford Budd; and as succeeding trustees Mr Edward Spencer, M.P., and the testator's brother, Mr Gamble North, are appointed. Col. North authorised the trustees to keep up, with a view to beneficial realisation, his racing and breeding establishments (including his greyhounds as well as his horses); and he also authorised the trustees to apply any part of the capital of his estate to carry on and develop, with a view to realisation, any projects and under- takings in which he might be engaged, and to keep up his establishment at Avery hill for three months after his death. He bequeathed to his son Harry absolutely his jewellery and for life his presentation plate, which is to be in trust for his son Harry's eldest or only son. Colonel North bequeathed*

*to his wife £ 10,000, and such plate and furniture to the value of £2,000 and such horses and carriages to the value of £ 500 as she might select. He bequeathed to his sister Emma Taylor £ 5,000, to her daughters Louisa Maud Dickinson and Florence Pratt £ 2,500 each; to his niece Emma Mary Beasley £ 5,000, to her children Beatrice and Mavin £ 2,500 each to Rose (daughter of his deceased brother Harry North) £2,500 to each child of his brother Gamble North £2,500, and to his said brother any sum which might be due from him to the testator. Col. North states in his will that all presents made by him to his children in his lifetime are to be in addition to the provisions made for them by his will, and having made valuable presents to his wife, he expresses the wish that she shall within six months provide that after her death they shall be inherited by his children. He leaves his residuary estate in trust to set apart sufficient and only sufficient" to pay one-fourth of the income to Mrs North during her life "if and only if" she so long remains his widow, and he leaves one other fourth share to his son Harry, one other fourth part upon trust for his daughter Emma, and the remaining one fourth in trust to apply the income for the benefit of his son Arthur Jewell North until he attains the age of 21 years, and to pay him one moiety of his share, and to pay the income of the other moiety to him until the age of 28 years, and then to pay this moiety also to him. The trustees are authorised to invest upon the security of landed estate in the United Kingdom.'*

The will mentions *'his sister Emma Taylor'* – North's sister Emma's second husband was an Andrew Taylor, John Dickinson having died of tuberculosis in 1883. It also mentions *'to his niece Emma Mary Beasley £ 5,000, to her children Beatrice and Mavin £2,500 each'.* Emma Mary is Mary Emma on the 1891 Census and there is another daughter Naomi Beasley who is not mentioned in the will.

It seems there was not much left in the coffers, considering North had been dubbed '*one of the richest men in the world*' not that long before he died – but then neither had he lost everything in the nitrate market downturn, as some had claimed. Maybe that was all just so much *tabloid sensationalism.*

**On 27ᵗʰ July 1896 Wilkinson & Son** held an auction of The Avery Hill estate in three lots; the freehold Mansion house and grounds of 143 acres and two adjoining leasehold properties; Pippinhall Farm (430 acres) and Avondale (24acres). Pippinhall, which took in *Rye Field Style, Shepherds Leys Wood, Coal Pits Wood, Upper and Lower Rennets, Reston's Woods* and part of *Oxley's Wood,* is described as having a brick and timber-built farm house and two brick-built and slated cottages, as well as two other dwellings *Crown Manor Cottage* and a keeper's cottage known as *Crown Cottage,* which came with *the right of shooting over the estate.* Avondale was described as comprising a '*Capital Residence*' and '*Pretty Pleasure Garden'.*

The sale catalogue described Avery Hill itself as an '*Important and Valuable Freehold Residential Estate*', an '*Excellent Family Mansion*' with a '*Noble Picture Gallery or Ball Room'.*

Sevenoaks Chronicle and Kentish Advertiser 31ˢᵗ July 1896:-

> '*AVERY HILL AUCTION. The estate of the late Colonel North, situated in Kent, was put up to auction in London on Monday. The property was divided into three lots— Avery-hill, Pippenhall Farm, and Avondale—the purchaser of lot one have the option of securing lots two and three at a fixed price. The auctioneer, in submitting the property, stated that Avery Hill cost between £200,000 and £260,000 to erect and lay out. The only bid forthcoming was one of £60,000, and Avery Hill was withdrawn as reserve of £100,000.*'

A tragic outcome for the Colonel's *dream* house. There were cries that the Mansion was a *white elephant*, despite rumours that the Duke of York may have been a potential purchaser.

The London Evening Standard of 15<sup>th</sup> March 1898 held this account of the Wilkinson auction of the Mansion contents:-

> *'SALE AT AVERY HILL HALL. COLONEL NORTH'S RACING PLATE. The contents of the residence of the late Colonel J. T. North, including the racing trophies and pictures, were yesterday submitted to sale by auction, on the first of five days over which the sale will extend. Avery Hill was for fourteen years the residence of Colonel North, who added very materially to the original dwelling, until the mansion became capable of accommodating a large number of guests. Messrs. G. A. Wilkinson and Son, of the Poultry, were entrusted with the sale, and the senior partner officiated yester- day in the picture gallery, where the auction was held. There was a very large attendance. The portions sold were from the corridor, back bed-rooms, ground floor, entrance hall, morning and dining rooms, and the racing plate and plate and plated good, used by the family.'*

The Mansion along with seven and a half acres, was eventually sold by Wilkinson's in June 1898 for the knock-down price of £40,000, to a Dr. Alonzo Stocker, a leading psychiatrist of the day, who intended to turn it into a luxurious asylum for the well-heeled, who were always in the market for places of genteel incarceration for their unwanted members. The Victorians were very keen on these institutions, especially for the detention of *hysterical* females. Stocker already had a London house, *Ashley Gardens* in Westminster as well as a country retreat *Craigwell House* in Aldwick near Bognor Regis, so it seems unlikely he intended living at Avery Hill himself.

For whatever reason, Stocker's plans did not materialise and sadly the house remained empty for a further eight years until it was again put up for auction. Eight years of neglect in which the house would have suffered from being empty.

**Hampton & Sons auction of Avery Hill on 30ᵗʰ July 1901 (catalogue with photographs)**

Dr. Stocker eventually sold the house and twenty eight acres of parkland to the LCC (London County Council, forerunner to the also defunct Greater London Council) in 1902 for an unbelievable £25,000, not far off what the Colonel had originally paid for the house before embarking on his *'renovations'*. It was acquired by the LCC without their having decided exactly what it should be utilised for. Jill Franklin laments the fate of many country houses like Avery Hill, built for the privileged way of life of their owners, which only a few decades after being built were becoming a burden, with many left to decay and some being demolished or painfully or unsuitably adapted, as Avery Hill would.

The LCC Parks Committee had estimated annual maintenance of Avery Hill at £3,000, but incredibly, this figure DID NOT include maintenance of the Mansion itself – a serious oversight.

On 25ᵗʰ May 1903 Avery Hill was opened as a public park by Lord Monkswell Chairman of the LCC, in front of a crowd of thousands and at this point the intention was that the grounds and the lower floor of the house should be open for the use of the public on Thursdays and Saturdays, with refreshments being offered by a Mr. Hendry who already had the contract to supply the same at the nearby *Rangers House* on Blackheath, while the upper floors would be used as a convalescent home for children. Lord Monkswell declared:-

> *'The County Council believe, not only in meeting present requirements, but in anticipating those of a succeeding generation'.*

And on those grounds he claimed that the purchase of Avery Hill was thoroughly justified.

Given the current (2018) impasse between UOG and Greenwich Council regarding Avery Hill's future, local residents can only wish they had public figures like Lord Monkswell who might see themselves as custodians of this precious legacy for future generations.

Various possible uses were considered, with each eventually being rejected as unsuitable: concert venue and art gallery, horticultural training centre for unemployed youth, convalescent home. However, it was the council's intention that the public should have access to the Sculpture Gallery, Ballroom/Picture Gallery and one of the drawing rooms. It soon became clear that the fabric of the Mansion had suffered from eight years without occupants – it is quite shocking to reflect that the house was still only 12 years old at this time!!. The roofs of the Ballroom and Sculpture Gallery required urgent repair and more seriously, it was discovered that the original roof construction was problematic, in that in hot weather the iron girders supporting it (Raffles-Davison account tells us 70 tons of it), expanded cracking the cement. It also required asphalting to make it water-tight. What had been the Colonel's *state-of-the-art* electricity generating system in 1890 had fallen well behind in the technological advances in that sphere in the intervening decade and £700 had to be spent immediately in updating it. The wiring was serviceable but the Cornish boiler, horizontal compound engine and rope-driven dynamo were obsolete with the accumulators (batteries) and switchboard being even more decrepit. So extensive was the problem that the LCC toyed with the idea of scrapping the system entirely and connecting the Mansion to the local grid, but on investigation this would have proved too expensive so they mended and made do. It was far from adequate and on dark winter days during its time as a ladies college, lessons would continue to be conducted in semi-darkness until the Mansion was finally connected to the grid in the 1930's.

Shorney states that with all this in mind, the Parks Committee was not sorry to relinquish responsibility to the Education Committee in 1904. This has echoes as I write in 2018 with both Greenwich Council and

UOG wanting to buck-pass responsibility for the fragile Mansion site in the light of expensive maintenance work which Historic England has declared must be undertaken.

Avery Hill was then opened in 1906 as the LCC's first residential teachers training college for women students within the London Education Area. Shorney suggests that although the Mansion was a showpiece of Victorian extravagance, as an educational establishment it had many shortcomings – much the same sort of observation that is being levelled at one of the current (Nov 2018) plans to have a Harris Academy Boys School at the Mansion site. Shorney also observes that facilities for sport at Avery Hill were limited as the College had a minimal amount of land, insufficient for hockey-pitches or tennis courts, it was as he says '*a college within a public park*' and as such lacked privacy, again much the same sort of objections being levelled at the current plan for a boy's academy on the site, and that is without the very real security and health and safety implications.

From 1906-1922 the Mansion accommodated between forty to fifty live-in students in cramped but magnificently located dormitories at the top of the marble staircase in what would have been the bedrooms during the North's time. Privacy and space may have been minimal – these dormitories looked much like a hospital ward with curtains separating each cubicle, but the young women seem to have been happy with the trade-off between comfort and spectacular surroundings.

In 1908 the LCC was able to acquire another grand site at a knockdown price, the 13 acres comprising *Southwood House* and surrounding grounds, which was destined to become the College's Halls of Residence. Mr. J.J. Smith, who had lived in this highly *Victorianised* Georgian house since 1875 and was a friend and business associate of Colonel Norths's, put it up for sale and the LCC bought it for just £6,000. What is now Avery Hill Road was at this time known as Southwood Road and was still little more than a country lane which disappeared into dense woodland to the south and east with *Southwood House* sitting on the edge giving it a sense of seclusion and remoteness.

Shorney writes, that what struck the first intake of Avery Hill students, was not what we might view now as extremely restrictive regulation, but the absence of domestic restraint, having come from typically regimented middle class Edwardian homes. They delighted in their freedom to saunter in the surrounding grounds or just indulge in some quiet contemplation in the conservatories during free periods. They were dazzled by the opulence and splendour of their new surroundings, deriving as much pleasure from the beautiful parkland that lay on their doorstep as they did from their magnificent Mansion. The glory of the autumnal colours of the creepers covering the house was particularly inspirational in the early days of the College. For many students, this was an adventure for which they would remain profoundly thankful for the rest of their days. '*The college is a magnificent place*' wrote one student to her cousin in 1907.

David Shorney writes of a reporter for The Eltham and District Times of 19th June 1914, who, having visited the college concluded:-

> '*Students now have the pleasure of working among surroundings designed for the pleasure of a millionaire. They go to lectures up a marble staircase which cost £20,000; they walk into a palatial dining room under an onyx arch which cost £10,000; and they can chat about lawn tennis while strolling up and down one of the finest marble halls in the country.....they drill in a banqueting chamber fit for a king*'

Students who were lucky enough to have bedrooms in the Eastern Tower, were rewarded with late evening, moonlit-bathed views of the surrounding fields and parkland.[1]

After suffering slight bomb damage in 1941, the fabric of the house remained exposed to the elements, and when the college returned from evacuation in 1947, it soon became clear that an awful lot of money would need to be expended on a property which had remained empty for some 8 years. Many accounts I have read mistakenly suggest that it was bomb damage that destroyed the eastern section of the mansion, but it was in fact years of neglect during and after the war. Valuable quantities of sugar and butter were being stored in the mansion during the war and when the incendiary bomb struck, the college Engineer, a Mr. Bennett, who had stayed behind when the college evacuated to the north of England, was quick to act, along with fire-wardens, in putting the fire out. However as a result of this fire-fighting, water damage had ruined the intricate plaster ceilings and many of these were now unsafe for the return of the students. In addition, mould had penetrated the tapestried walls and an attack of fungus lifted the oak paneling and parquet and the intricate mosaic flooring. The council's architect concluded in December 1945 that *Most of the features which give the College/Mansion a certain character, have now disappeared*.[2]

And so, tragically, it was decided that two thirds of the house should be demolished, including the whole of the eastern section, with the loss of the dining-room, billiard-room, morning room, three-roomed Turkish Bath and the East Gallery. Edmundson states that the Eastern Wing was *destroyed* during WWII and that this part was rebuilt in 1958 but in a different *style*. In my opinion, what has been rebuilt bears no comparison with the original structure as this is a utilitarian educational building grafted onto the remaining structure with nothing linking them.

Miraculously, the ornate gentleman's Lavatory survived this desecration, although now designated a *Ladies* (blog *listed ladies loo opened to visitors* 2010). Designated Grade II Listed are:- Gents Lavatory, the Entrance Gate and Lodge, lobby passage (Sculpture Gallery), theatre (Picture Gallery) and Conservatory (Winter Garden).

Conservation work on the Winter Garden in 2010 focused on the glasshouse and the pool area and also saw an attempt to restore the planting style from North's day, with the re-introduction of flowers and plants from Chile along with the usual cacti and exotic trees taking their place alongside the 60ft+ Canary Island Palms.

What a tragic outcome for a house, that a little creative thinking from Greenwich Council, might have restored the Mansion as a valuable community asset, after all, when it was originally re-opened in 1903 by the LCC, it was intended that the grounds and the lower floor, be opened to the public.

Sadly, this gem of high-Victorianism, remains all but hidden from the public gaze and this must change. If this account can inspire readers to visit Avery Hill and perhaps notice the interwoven JTN initials amongst the wrought iron entrance gates or maybe raise their eyes to see the eagle with its claws above the stone with '1890' atop the entrance doorway, then I have achieved something. I was eager to know more of the Colonel and his house and there was very little information available. I am neither a historian nor an experienced writer, but having embarked on finding out as much as possible, I wanted to collate my findings for the benefit of others who may be fired with a similar curiosity to know more of *Colonel North and his Nitrate Dream House*.

## Avery Hill – the Present and the Future

*Save Avery Hill Winter Garden Campaign*

A petition to Save Avery Winter Garden was started due to the concerns of local residents that UOG were not honouring their responsibility to maintain the structure – the Grade II listed site was on English Heritage's *at risk* register. This pressure group has been set up to draw attention to the plight of this unique community asset and campaigners say the university, which announced plans to sell the Winter Garden and surrounding teaching facilities in December 2014, is threatening to leave the adjacent Mansion boarded up when it vacates the building at the end of 2018, although apparently (according to Councillor Fahy)

**the covenant covering the Winter Garden states that it must be kept open to the public for 364 days of the year.** The Winter Garden forms part of the Mansion garden and is said to be the largest temperate winter garden in the country after Kew Gardens. SAWG say that while UOG are just doing basic repairs, the Winter Garden needs £6m spent to renovate and £750,000 to turn the Picture Gallery into a usable *arts space* and also ask that the £3m lottery bid abandoned by UOG be resurrected, but do not venture to suggest by whom.

Already, large areas of the structure are in a poor state of repair, and neighbours are fearing for the building's future. Campaigners say the stalemate is down to a disagreement over what to with the building, which the university bought from Greenwich Council for £1 in 1992.

Many of the university's teaching facilities on the site have moved to a new home in Greenwich, and it abandoned a lottery bid aimed at restoring the Winter Garden after deciding to leave.

While the university had hoped to build some housing on the site, the council is said to be insisting it stays in educational use – reportedly wanting to relocate a secondary school on the site. Campaigners say it is unlikely a secondary school could raise the funds needed to restore the Winter Garden.

### As at March 2018

Currently scaffolding around the Winter Garden to facilitate repairs to the roof (100 glass panels replaced) which were required by *Historic England*, following a site visit, to prevent further deterioration prior to potential sale to Harris Academy for use as a boys secondary school, although quite why there is the need for another secondary school with the relatively new and enlarged Crown Woods Academy just across the road. Greenwich Council have agreed to a new lottery bid but campaigners fear there is no proper plan and that Harris's involvement may compromise any renovation works on the Gardens and Mansion.

## David Shorney interview in SEnine Magazine April 2018 edition

David remembers the Winter Garden being in well-kept condition when he arrived in 1974 (I remember it being in not too bad a condition when I first saw it in the early 1990's). He says the University of Greenwich should be censured for '*allowing the plants to die and* the *building to rot*'. After the abolition of the GLC in 1986, responsibility for the park and Winter Garden passed to the London Borough of Greenwich and all the expertise of those looking after the Winter Garden was lost. He wrote his book '*Teachers in training': A History of Avery Hill College*' as he '*wanted to convey an accurate picture of life there because I found many grammar schools were less than complimentary about teachers trained at Avery Hill*', even though many went on to be head teachers, school inspectors and community leaders.

'*It's a unique and priceless asset and I hope the gardens and the buildings will be completely restored*'. **David Shorney**

As Jill Franklin had said in '*The English Country House…*':-

'*but perhaps in the end we shall come to feel that we must not part with all of this legacy of weird and evocative buildings*'.

### From sammaccauley's blog:-

'*The critical point is that there is no current obligation on the University or the potential Developer to restore the listed buildings, only to maintain them. Only if the site is converted into a premium hospitality space, would there be a "business case" to restore the site. However, it would require a bold business — even with the support of Lottery Funding — to invest millions of pounds to restore these buildings to commercialise them as a hotel, restaurant, or wedding venue. Also what would happen to the public access covenant if the Winter Garden was a commercial venture?*'

**Site registered an Asset of Community Value.** The following from the local NewsShopper paper dated 15th June 2018:-

*Campaign to Save Avery Hill Winter Garden takes huge step to rescue 'architectural gem'*

*'A campaign to save an abandoned architectural gem in a leafy corner of Eltham has taken a big step to save the building.*

*The 19 century Avery Hill Winter Gardens has been registered as an Asset of Community Value after a petition garnered thousands of signatures saying it was worth saving.*

*Terry Powley, from the campaign group, said it showed how much local residents care about the winter garden.*

*He said: "It is clearly a local community asset, and the community should play a major part in deciding its future.*

*"It's very encouraging that the council has given the site this protected status, but with the University set to move out in six months, the clock is ticking, and we need urgent action to secure its future."*

*The Winter Garden in Avery Hill Park is capable of containing tropical trees and plants year round, but it has been derelict for years with broken windows and water running down the walls. While it is technically open to the public, campaigners have said nobody would realistically want to visit them in their current state.*

*The building is currently owned by the University of Greenwich, alongside an old art gallery next door that is used as a library, and the university agreed to sell the site in 2014.*

*Councillor Nigel Fletcher, who represents* **Eltham South ward** *on Greenwich Council, has been supporting the cross-party campaign.*

*He said: "Local residents have demonstrated very clearly how much they value the Winter Garden as a community asset, so it's only right it now has that formal status.*

*"Thousands signed the petition in favour of restoration, and we've had huge support at public meetings on the issue.*

*"Getting this important part of our heritage properly restored is a personal priority for me, and I will continue pressing the Council and the University to work constructively with the campaign group to achieve that. It has huge potential, but we need commitment from all parties to make it happen."*

*'alongside an old art gallery' I was wondering what they were referring to, when I realised that it was the Colonel's magnificent Picture Gallery – Philistines!*

## 21st Oct 2019 – Public Meeting at Eltham Warren Golf Club

Attended by local councillors and residents and chaired by SAWG. Established that UOG have sold the Avery Hill Mansion site, minus the Winter Garden, to Harris Academy. The Winter Garden has reverted to the responsibility of Greenwich Council with a dowry for its upkeep from UOG from the proceeds of the sale – only fitting seeing as they bought the whole site from Greenwich Council for £1!!. Main concerns voiced:-

• Unsuitability of the site for a secondary school – potential rivalry with Crown Woods. Security issues with Mansion being a school and attached Winter Garden having public access.

- Is another 1000 pupil secondary school necessary with 2000 pupil Crown Woods just across the road? Apparently there i*s a curr*ent surplus of 500 secondary boy's school places.

- Parking is already a major issue for local residents.

- Sundering of the connection between Mansion and Winter Garden with *subsequent loss of* the processional route.

- Resurrect the Lottery Bid. Possibility of housing not entirely abandoned

A covenant covering the Winter Garden, states that it must be kept open to the public for 364 days of the year. I added that it had always been the intention of the Council that parts of the Mansion and Winter Garden would be open to the public and quoted Lord Monkswell when opening Avery Hill in 1903:-

> *'The County Council believe, not only in meeting present requirements, but in anticipating those of a succeeding generation'.*

**UOG will finally be vacating the Mansion site in April 2020**

# Additional Information

North Graves in Eltham Churchyard (St. John's)

Determined to seek these out, I proceeded to make my way towards the largest monument in the cemetery, as I was told this marked the North graves. This was a very dangerous undertaking as the ground became very uneven and overgrown, with fallen headstones hidden by the long grass and deep gullies where the ground had sunk, I soon became aware of the folly of my undertaking but I was determined to get a closer look at the memorial. The closer I got, the worse the ground became, I could just about decipher that I was looking at the *North* memorial (pink marble, with grey marble urn which must have sat on the top but was now resting on its side in the grass). The *Blenkiron* memorial next to it is marked by a tall thin obelisk and both seem to be enclosed by rusting railings and so completely engulfed in brambles that it was impossible to get close enough to accurately decipher the inscriptions. A truly sad spectacle. While I was trying to take some pictures on my phone, a lady PCSO approached and asked what I was doing. I knew she must have thought I was up to no good as I remembered that a few weeks previously there was lots of police activity, with many marked and unmarked cars with sirens blaring, all centred around this churchyard. The officer explained that there was ongoing gang activity at the McDonalds which is just across the road, and gang members were hiding weapons in the churchyard – they would be unarmed for a *stop-and-search*, but only had to cross the road to pick up their previously stashed knives. I said that I might try and get a group of volunteers to help clear these sadly neglected memorials, the PCSO suggested that this would be a good project for those criminals doing *Community Service,* but we both agreed this would not be allowed as the criminals might injure themselves on the brambles!! What a crazy world we are living in. She did seem genuinely interested in the subject of my search, Colonel North, but she had not seen Avery Hill. A sad final resting place for an Eltham resident who was reputed to be '*one of the richest men in the world*', so renowned that he has not even been remembered with a bench in the High Street.

## Hotel Metropole

The images of the Hotel Metropole showing what looks like a huge battleship, confused me as I assumed the picture was taken from the Trafalgar Square end but it is actually taken from the Embankment looking towards Trafalgar Square. The tall triangular building is the Hotel Metropole, with the Whitehall Rooms opening out upon Whitehall Place, on the left. Beyond the Metropole in Northumberland Avenue, is the Hotel Victoria. The not unattractive building to the right of our picture (See Image 13 above), is the Avenue Theatre, bounded by Craven Street, leading to the Strand, and by the road leading under Charing Cross Railway Bridge. Northumberland Avenue takes its name from the town house of the *Percy* family, which, having been bought by the Metropolitan Board of Works, was removed in 1874 to make room for *improvements* at this spot.

The Hotel Metropole was designed by Frederick Gordon (owner of a chain of Metropole hotels) and constructed between 1883 and 1885. By the turn of the 20th century Hotel Metropole had become one of the most popular hotels in London. In 1936, it was leased to the Government to provide temporary accommodation for various departments. The building was sold by the *Crown Estates* in 2007 and reopened in 2011 as part of the 5 Star *Corinthia Hotel London.* Its location, just by Charing Cross Station made it popular with both Londoners and foreign travellers arriving on the boat-train from Europe. Prince Albert, later King Edward VII, was a regular visitor to the hotel, having a reserved box in the ballroom and entertaining guests in the Royal Suite, thought to have been the first floor rooms with bow-fronted windows fronting Whitehall Place. With such provenance it was eminently suitable for Col. North's lavish entertainments while he awaited the completion of his Mansion. It was also ideally placed for the many theatres and restaurants which this area was noted for, both of which North was very partial to.

## John Oliver Cook 1852-1925 (successor to T.W.Cutler in overseeing the building of Avery Hill)

Cook was born at *Bostall Farm* in Plumstead, his family subsequently moved to nearby *Moreton Villa,* by which time 'Ollie', as he was known in the family, was 17 years old and articled to Mr. H.H. Church of 'Church & Rickwood Architects & Surveyors' of 44, William St, Woolwich. He later branched out on his own, his main work being for *Beasley's Brewery,* for whom he oversaw the rebuilding (possibly even the original building) of *The Bull Hotel* on Shooter's Hill – there is a prominent date-stone stating *Rebuilt 1881* with Cook's name as architect – he was also possibly involved with the building of the nearby *Red Lion* also. In addition he undertook numerous commissions for factories, these proving very lucrative. He was designated *architect* of the Woolwich High Schools and Surveyor to the Woolwich Union (Workhouse?), but the bulk of his work seems to have been *maintenance* rather than *design*. On marrying in 1879, he and his wife took up residence at the newly-built *North End Villa*, No 2, Wrottesley Rd. and remained there for the rest of their lives. Mears tells an alarming story of the Cook children, J.O. walking and Christian (unusual for a girl, but a family name) being wheeled in a pram, up Plum Lane to Shrewsbury Lane all of which was very rustic at this time with open parkland. Four year-old J.O Junior would take pot-shots with his air-gun at rooks in the surrounding trees, then piling the corpses on the pram cover! Sounds like a scene from a Gothic horror-film!

## T.W. Cutler Hotel Metropole Folkestone

This building is still standing. As a hotel it could accommodate 300+ guests but has recently been converted into flats. Cutler was the architect and the hotel opened in 1896 having cost, at £150,000, according to

Image 31; Metropole Folkestone

The Builder July 31st 1897 pg 92, perhaps half what Avery Hill did six years previously (and it's got marble columns too!).

Cutler died in Dec 1909 having lived at 5, Queens Square in Bloomsbury. In addition, he had been involved in the rebuilding in 1900-02 of the *Bull and Mouth Hotel* near Briggate in Leeds. Cutler was, like many architects, an accomplished artist and his drawings of the Sculpture Gallery, East Gallery, Dining Room, Visitors Staircase and Turkish Bath at Avery Hill were exhibited at the Royal Academy between 1890-3.

### Burmantofts Faience

I am including this description as the term was used in descriptions of the Lavatory and Garden Court, without clarification as to what exactly it was.

The Burmantofts business began in 1859, when fire clay was discovered in a coal mine owned by William Wilcock and John Lassey. In 1863 Lassey's share was bought by John Holroyd and the company then named Wilcock & Co.

In 1879, after a period of expansion, the firm made decorative bricks and tiles in orange or buff-coloured architectural terracotta, glazed bricks, and glazed terracotta (faience). Architect Alfred Waterhouse used their materials in his *Yorkshire College* (1883) in Leeds, which is now the *University of Leeds* and whose *Great Hall* is one of the best surviving examples of *Burmantofts* decoration, and his National Liberal Club (1884) in London. From 1880 they also made art pottery such as vases and decorative domestic items.

In 1888 the company was renamed *The Burmantofts Company* but in 1889 it merged with other Yorkshire companies to found *The Leeds Fireclay Co. Ltd.*, the largest in the country.

James Holroyd the works manager now realised that a more decorative version of the company's salt-glazed bricks could be useful as an architectural facing material which could be easily cleaned of the grime of industrial cities and was more permanent than paint. Simple coloured tiles or bricks were complemented by relief patterns, and a variety of glazes. However, the fashion for highly modelled surfaces had passed by the turn of the century and the company closed in 1957.

Examples:-

- Atlas House, King Street, Leeds
- County Arcade, Leeds (Frank Matcham)
- Great Hall interior, University of Leeds, 1890–94, (Alfred Waterhouse)
- Michelin House, South Kensington, London
- National Liberal Club, London
- London Road Fire Station, Manchester

## Turkish Bath at Gledhow Hall , Roundhay Leeds

Image 32; Gledhow Hall Turkish Bath

I came across this picture of a Turkish Bath, while searching the internet for pictures of the interior of the renovated Avery Hill. This seemed to be very much in the style of that at Avery Hill with its extensive use of *Burmantofts faience*. Imagine my dismay when I found that it was in what had once been the home of the Kitson family, contemporaries of North's in his metal-bashing days in Leeds. In '*The Life and Career of the Late Col. North*' published in Leeds in 1896, North claims to have worked for the company for 12s a week, with some accounts claiming it was work for Kitsons that first took him to Chile.

The Hall, now converted to flats, was completed shortly after 1766, by John Carr for John Beckett; altered and extended for James Kitson, Lord Airedale c1885-1890 by architects Chorley and Connon. Lord Airedale (1835-1911) was the 2nd son of James Kitson (1807-85), founder of the famous Kitson Airedale locomotive foundries, in close proximity to where the young North lived at Grape Street. It was James Kitson who commissioned the impressive hand-painted Burmantofts "faience" tile bathroom, designed for a visit by the Prince of Wales (later Edward VII) in 1885. An industrial magnate and notable figure in the Liberal party locally and nationally; he was created baronet in 1887. The Middleton family connection with Gledhow begins in 1875 when the Gledhow Wood Estate was purchased by German nobleman – Edward, Baron von Schunck – who had married Kate Lupton in 1867. Kate, the daughter of a former Mayor of Leeds and whose descendant Olive Middleton, was the great grandmother of Kate Middleton now Duchess of Cambridge.

## Tynecastle Tapestry

This is another decorative material mentioned in descriptions of the Mansion, without an explanation of what exactly it was.

In 1881-82, William Scott Morton undertook a short study tour of Italy, where he became impressed by Spanish and Italian leather hangings. Not long after his return, an elderly London leatherworker turned up seeking employment, and after much experiment Morton

& Co developed Tynecastle Canvas or *Tynecastle Tapestry*. This was an embossed leather-like material compound of canvas and paste, which could be aged, tinted and gilded. Its success resulted in a huge order for Young's Glasgow City Chambers, and another for the redecoration of the picture galleries at Grosvenor House for the Duke of Westminster. To meet the demand for this material, and for the embossed canvas plaster friezes that had been patented by Morton & Co in 1885, John and James Templeton became partners in The Tynecastle Company.

**Campbell Smith & Co** *(responsible for most of the stained-glass windows at Avery Hill)*

From their website:-

> 'Since 1873, the name of Campbell Smith & Co Ltd has been synonymous with expert advice and experienced consultancy services, united with the highest quality of craftsmanship. Our project list includes many National Monuments, Palaces and Houses, Museums and Galleries, Cathedrals and Churches, as well as modern buildings requiring fine decoration with traditional skill and care.'

I contacted them as it was their company which produced many of the stained-glass windows for Avery Hill (including those in the Lavatory) and their Mr. Smith had painted the exquisite looking *sepia cartoons* (See Image 25 above), overlooking the stairwell of the Marble Staircase, the only image of which I have come across was in The British Architect of 17th Jan 1890 and these images have a large band running across the middle. I was hoping that they might have something in their company archives, but was told that most of those dating to the 19thC were lost.

**Dr. Alonzo Stocker / Ashley Gardens**

On Sun 11th Nov 2018, I was making my way towards a Remembrance Sunday service at St Matthews Church in Westminster. I knew there would be tight security at Westminster Underground station, due to the service at the Cenotaph, but did not expect to find the whole area cordoned off and hence my route down Embankment, past the Houses of Parliament blocked. I decided to take the Circle Line to Victoria and approach from that direction. I knew the general direction I needed to be going in, so I proceeded down Victoria St and then turned right at Westminster Cathedral, and there was the looming mansion block of Ashley Gardens on my left, so if the dates proved correct Dr Stocker's London home was actually in a block of flats, albeit grand ones. Subsequent enquiry showed that Ashley Gardens built in 1890, was the first of such blocks, which the upper and middle classes at this time found to be eminently suited to their modern way of living as R. Phené Spiers, sometime Master of the Architectural School, Royal Academy, London], in Encyclopædia Brittanica, 11th ed. (Cambridge: University Press, 1910) observed:-

> *"Perhaps in one respect the greatest change which has been made in the English house is the adoption of 'flats'; commenced..... in Ashley Gardens, Westminster, they have spread throughout London....The increasing demand for these, however, shows that they meet, so far as their accommodation and comfort are concerned, the wants and tastes of the upper and middle classes"*

Extracts from *"The World of the New: The First Ten Years"*, by Valerie Kingman.: Ashley Gardens Residents Association, 1990:-

> *Ashley Gardens ... offered a very different London lifestyle, central and convenient, generous in accommodation and advanced in design. Who would move in? Who would be able to tolerate the appalling noise and dirt associated with the construction of a Cathedral, a Roman Catholic cathedral at that and of enormous proportions, next door? Of course, for many these innovative developments offered a pleasant alternative for families living mainly in the country: husbands and fathers could reduce London expenses and entertaining in reasonable style: space was provided for domestic servants."*

*"Ashley Gardens, as it was completed, rapidly established its social importance. Kelly's Directory for the 1890s indicates that tenants were happy to move in as the blocks were completed, some even being tempted from other new developments. Block 1 was virtually full by the end of 1890 with blocks 2 and 5 following in occupation by the end of 1891. ... All the blocks attracted pretty well the same social mix; MPs, army and navy officers, medical doctors and lawyers pursuing their careers were the neighbors of a large number clearly living on reasonable private means."*

**Further development surrounding Avery Hill**

The Crown sold 68 acres of neighbouring farmland for development in 1936. Several builders collaborated in laying out a set of streets which are now known as the Eltham Heights Estate. These new streets took their names from the fields and woods that they replaced – Crown Woods (Crown Woods Way), Rye Field (Riefield Rd) Coal Pits Woods (Colepits Wood Rd). After the war the LCC took over and completed the estate, building a school and blocks of flats, to the annoyance of some early residents. The GLC added a final phase, which included a nursery and retirement flats, before handing the estate over to the London Borough of Greenwich in 1980.

**Lemonwell**

Home of North's son Sir Harry (see Gregory). Henry received the knighthood which had sadly eluded his father, from King Edward VII in 1905. Harry died prematurely like his father, aged 53 in 1920. The name *Lemonwell* derived from the walled-well by the milestone on Bexley Rd opposite Gravel Pit Lane. It was considered by locals to have therapeutic (some thought *magical*) properties, especially for the eyes and according to RRC Gregory, this well was still in use in 1900. There seems to have been a significant house on the site of Lemonwell, as in 1888 it had a higher rateable value than the original Avery Hill house.

While he was rebuilding Avery Hill, Colonel North built two houses on the site where Lemonwell Drive now is. One was called *Lemonwell* which had the spring for the well in its grounds and this house was subsequently taken by North's son Harry, presumably on his marriage. Sadly, it was demolished in 1935 to make way for some less than picturesque council housing.

### Vale Mascal, Bexley

Built in 1740 and occupied in 1794 by Sir Francis Burdett MP and his wife Sophie (nee Coutts, daughter of banker Thomas Coutts. Vale Mascal Estate records have Arthur Jewell North here from 1911-49?? - this can't be right as Arthur Jewell was killed in action Sep 27th 1918 aged 34 – one of his five children Richard Arthur North born May 4th 1918 and died May 8th 1973 - 3 living North descendants:- Cecile Pelly, Sara Rawlings and William North (Herts?)

**Fred Shepherd**, North's grandson, still alive and living in Ireland as at May 1989

**Karen Lawrence** (quoted in Edmundson's book) whose husband is the great-grandson of Colonel North's niece Mary Emma Dickinson (daughter of his sister Emma)

David Shorney's notes mention Col North's grandson **Gary** or **Larry Pearman**, a keen point-to-pointer whose father was reputed to have drowned in a puddle- drunk!

*From blackfenthenandnow blog;-*

### Gamble North (J.T's brother) links with Blackfen

In fact Avery Hill has a link with Blackfen in its history. Avery Hill Mansion was created by Col John Thomas North 'Nitrate King' and the Winter Garden was completed in 1890. His brother, the mine engineer

Gamble North, was married (second marriage) to Leila, daughter of the tenant of Westwood Farm in Blackfen, John Hunt. After Col North died and his widow sold Avery Hill, Gamble North resided at Queens Wood, Blackfen – so maybe Gamble lived at Avery Hill for a time also.

The question is, of course: was the fertiliser produced by Col North's Chilean business used for the benefit of Westwood Farm?!

## Red Croft

On the corner of Tilt Yard (or Court Yard) and Court Rd, home of North's widow following move from Avery Hill. This was a much more modest middle-class type home and Jane North was probably relieved to be drastically downsizing given the upheaval of the Avery Hill renovations and the death of her husband.

## Holy Trinity Church Southend Crescent Eltham

This would have been the North's local church and Colonel and Mrs North's daughter Emma was married to George Alexander Lockett here in 1892. There are two commemorative plaques in what would have been the original entrance:-

TO THE GLORY OF GOD
FOR THE ENRICHMENT OF HIS SANCTUARY
AND IN EVER AFFECTIONATE
REMEMBRANCE
OF HER BELOVED HUSBAND COLONEL JOHN T.
NORTH
THE BAPTISTERY, NARTHEX AND
WEST WINDOW IN THIS CHURCH
WERE GIVEN BY
JANE NORTH
MDCCCCIX *(1909)*

The other an equally poignant remembrance to Barbara, the second daughter of '*Harry North Knight*' and his wife Jessie Louisa, who was '*Born, Baptised and Died*' March 1st 1910

The window given by Jane North is known as the *Kempe West Window*, after C E Kempe & Co. its maker, and depicts *Christ in Majesty* surrounded by angels. It is also known as the '*North*' window.

## Winter Garden as Film Location

The Winter Garden featured in two of Michael Winner's films to my knowledge. The 1965 *You Must be Joking* a comic spoof of an army training exercise, a sort of *treasure hunt* in which participants had to find various objects including a rare rose the *Lady Frances McDonaugh*, which was found in the Winter Garden (26 mins.in), which appears in full exotic foliage as it was still being well maintained by Greenwich Council at this time. A large sign at the entrance states '*Public Botanical Gardens Greenhouses and Hothouses 9am till Sunset*'. Whoever chose Winner's locations seems to have liked the Winter Garden as it was used again in the later 1978 film *The Big Sleep*, a murder/mystery starring Robert Mitchum, James Stewart and Sarah Miles. Just 5 minutes into the film *Philip Marlowe* (Robert Mitchum) meets the *General* (James Stewart) who is sitting in the Winter Garden in a leather armchair with a drinks table complete with telephone, beside him. Again, the garden is in splendid foliage looking like an Amazonian rainforest with its resplendent lush greenery. Sadly the Winter Garden in its current state of neglect does not seem to be in demand as a film location.

## Proctor Collection

Will Robley of UOG explained that he had personally delivered the Proctor Collection (Vera Proctor great-niece of Colonel North, granddaughter of his brother Gamble) which had been held in the college's archives, to the Abbey Museum in Leeds. Also the North Collection which seemed to consist solely of a North Family album of 1894 has been returned to the family along with portraits of Jane and Emma North which had hung in the Picture Gallery, while a digital copies of the contents are held by the UOG. How enchanted was I to learn that the UOG archives that I would be poring over, were located in the Minstrels Gallery!! So, I would be up there looking down onto the Ballroom/Picture Gallery, imagining what it might have been looked like with one of the Colonel's famous entertainments in full swing.

**Brian Howard Heaton** of 18, Palace Court, Sancroft St SE11 5UL was writing about North in about 1995, there is some correspondence between himself and RIBA in their Cutler biographical file.

*Nitrato de Chile*

Image 32; Gledhow Hall Turkish Bath

'*abonal con Nitrato de Chile*' seems to translate as '*fertilise with Nitrate from Chile*'

While on holiday in La Palma, Canary Islands, my son Nathan pointed out this image which seemed to be everywhere, on old street posters but especially on souvenirs and tee shirts. It is a strikingly good image and has lasted the test of time

This is the origin of the image (from Wikipedia);-

'*In 1909 two German scientists, **Fritz Haber** and **Carl Bosch,** worked out how to produce nitrogen chemically - in other words, how to artificially make nitrate on an industrial level.*

*In the years that followed, advertising for natural nitrate became increasingly important for the economic survival of the Chilean company whose product was **Nitrato de Chile**. In the early 1930s, Nitrato de Chile advertisements were made from ceramic tiles.*

*Advertising was in its infancy and the nitrate company placed thousands of the tile panels around rural Spain, often on the first house you pass when entering a village, the casilla de peones camineros (road workers' house), and on warehouses. They were carefully placed in both strategic and beautiful locations.*

*The image's designer was Adolfo López-Durán Lozano, from Madrid. While he was studying architecture, Lopez-Duran was asked to paint the advertisement by one of his teachers, who presumably had a connection with the Chilean nitrate company. What began as a kind gesture to support a student's financial situation ended up as being one of the most popular artistic icons of mid-20$^{th}$ century Spain.'*

### Bombing/Demolition

There are many accounts which give the impression that the whole of the East Wing was lost during WW2 bombing – there was slight bomb damage but the bulk of the damage was due to the following 7 years of neglect leading to demolition in 1947.

### John Oliver Cook

Cook, who was Cutler's assistant, took over when his boss was sacked by North. While Cook was not specifically referred to as an architect (except in Cook family memory where he was remembered as 'Colonel North's *architect*') the inference is natural that Cutler's successor was. Cook was actually what would now be called a Chartered Surveyor which accounts for my not being able to locate him at The Royal Institute of British Architects.

# Acknowledgements

My friend Ken Hampson, for his unstinting help preparing images, which nevertheless were still not up to his high standards

David Shorney for his comments, encouragement and of course his excellent book which I have quoted extensively

Eveleigh Bradford of the Thoresby Society (Leeds Local History) for information on the Norths in Leeds

Laurie Baker of the Eltham Society for tracking down Margaret Taylor's 'Road to South America' article from archives and other assistance rendered

Will Robley (Archivist Librarian) and his colleague Carla Butler of UOG at Avery Hill Mansion Site (due to move to Southwood Site April 2020)

Jonathan Partington in Search Room at Greenwich Heritage Centre (now closed)

Mark Hickson Secretary of the Blackheath Golf Club for showing me the North Scratch Medal

Joanna Stirling and members of the Eltham Writers Group

Staff at Royal Institute of British Architects (visited Nov 2018)

# Select Bibliography

Kristina Bedford 'Eltham Through Time' Amberley 2013

Arthur Binstead 'Pitcher in Paradise' Sands & Co. 1903

H. Blakemore article 'John Thomas North, The Nitrate King' History Today 1962

H. Blakemore 'British Nitrates and Chilean politics, 1886-1896: Balmaceda and North' 1974

J.B. Booth 'Palmy Days' The Richards Press 1957

Guy Deghy 'Paradise in the Strand : The Story of Romano's' The Richards Press 1958

William Edmundson 'The Nitrate King – A Biography of 'Colonel' John Thomas North' Palgrave 2011

Eltham Society 'Looking into Eltham' 1980 Margaret Taylor May 2008 walk 'The Road to South America'

Jill Franklin 'The Gentlemen's Country House and It's Plan 1835-1914' RKP 1981

R.R.C. Gregory 'The Story of Royal Eltham' 1909 Kentish District Times Co. Ltd

Thomas Hinde *'An Illustrated History of the University of Greenwich'* Univ. of Greenwich 2013

A. Hunting *'Avery Hill and It's Winter Garden'* Dissertation to Thames Polytechnic Faculty of Architecture Dec 1977

John Kennett *'Eltham in Old Photographs'* Alan Sutton 1993

John Mayo – *'Britain and Chile 1851-1886: Anatomy of a Relationship'* 1981

C.B. Mears Family Memoir *'The Cooks of Bostall'* written 1991

Rory Miller *'Britain and Latin America in the 19th and 20th centuries'* Longman 1993

William Howard Russell *'A Visit to Chile and The Nitrate Fields'* J. S. Virtue & Co 1890

Malcolm Shifrin *'Victorian Turkish Baths'* 2015

David Shorney *'Teachers in Training 1906-1985'* Thames Polytechnic 1989

David Sleep *'Images of London – Eltham'* Tempus 2004

Yorkshire Post article *'The Chemical Conquistador'* 13th Feb 2012

*'The Life and Career of The Late Colonel North as Told By Himself'*

*The King of Avery Hill* (Leeds Library Archive)

Printed in Poland
by Amazon Fulfillment
Poland Sp. z o.o., Wrocław

56200064R00125